A LOOK AT
FILIPINO LIFESTYLES

INTERNATIONAL MUSEUM OF CULTURES
PUBLICATION 8

Daniel W. Deyell
Museum Director

Desmond C. Derbyshire
Academic Publications Coordinator

A LOOK AT
FILIPINO LIFESTYLES

MARVIN K. MAYERS

INTERNATIONAL MUSEUM OF CULTURES

DALLAS, TEXAS

1984

© Summer Institute of Linguistics, Inc. 1980

Library of Congress Catalog Card Number: 79–91446

ISBN 0–88312–158–1

First edition 1980.

Cover design by Jerry Jenkins
Illustrations by Dave Beasley

This title available at:

The International Museum of Cultures
7500 W. Camp Wisdom Road
Dallas, TX   75236   U.S.A.

CONTENTS

Introduction 1

1. Making Contact with the Filipino 5
2. The Family 11
3. The Alliance 19
4. Linking Alliances 27
5. The Nation 33
6. Status 39
7. The Behavior of Status 47
8. Reciprocity 55
9. The Reciprocal Relationship 61
10. The Role of the Intermediary 73
11. Conflict and Conflict Resolution 79
12. Celebration 87
13. A Value Profile 91
14. Education 101
15. Orientation to Bicultural Living 113

Appendices
   1. A Survey of Philippine History 117
   2. History of Lipa City 126
Glossary 133
Bibliography 135

Acknowledgments

The Far Eastern Gospel Crusade helped make our stay in the Philippines possible. Our host couple, Romy and Zoriada Reyes, was very generous and can never be fully repaid nor can a number of special friends who made our first trip to the Philippines possible. Special appreciation is also expressed to the Tyndale Foundation for providing much of the funding for the initial and revised editions of this study.

My wife's untiring efforts in the field and at home in preparing and typing the manuscript were of tremendous benefit and greatly appreciated. Don and Gwen Douglas, Crusade personnel, were of special help in my research. Don had had adequate preparation for Far Eastern study and I could not possibly have gone this deeply into the analytic work had it not been for his training and insight.

Miss Carol Herrmann researched extensively the archives of the Philippine Study Program of the Department of Anthropology at the University of Chicago and assisted in the writing of Chapter 8. Carol Snarey wrote the survey history of the Philippines. Mr. and Mrs. Ceferino Villegas, Miss Elisa Espinelli and Benjamín de Jesús assisted me in expanding the field data. They have been a great help in evaluating the material itself, and in providing the alternative approaches which are incorporated in this study. Their insights enriched and completed my own experience with the Filipino culture. John Snarey compiled the bibliography and notes and references. Marilyn Olson and Vendla Walton have worked untiringly to edit and rewrite portions of the present revision.

Introduction

This volume is designed as a manual for the North American entering the Philippines. It attempts to do several things: it presents information concerning points of greatest potential conflict between the two cultures; it organizes Filipino culture into conceptual models so that the North American can gain clarity, insight and an effective perspective about this valid society; and it shows the importance of working within the society's system to insure satisfactory interpersonal relationships and to accomplish desired goals.

In March of 1969, my wife and I were asked to study Filipino culture and lifestyles with the idea of promoting a better understanding of the culture and ways of living and working within it. We planned to live in a provincial Filipino culture and as our studies progressed we would hold seminars to communicate our observations and recommendations.

A young couple of the upper status were our hosts. They had recently built a home in a new subdivision of Lipa City. Our host was an attorney employed by the Rural Development Bank and the Lipa Electric Company as legal counsel. He also carried on private law practice at home. His wife worked part-time at the Court of First Instance as interpreter. Both spoke English. They had four young children and four house girls. Three of the house girls attended school part-time.

My wife and I both had had extensive training and field experience in anthropology and linguistics. We had spent thirteen years in Latin America learning one expression of the same cultural background as the Philippines. Though we did little reading prior to entering the Philippines, we immersed ourselves in the written materials about that country from the day we arrived. We followed this practice characteristic of social anthropologists so that what we read would expand our knowledge about the culture, and not prebias us causing us to see things not there or to overlook significant aspects of the culture.

Since our host couple was of high status within the society, the entire society and its culture were open to us. Had we lived in a lower status home, only the characteristics of the lower statuses would have been opened to us.

During our stay in Lipa City, we made use of the following anthropological research techniques:

• *Participant observation.* We kept our eyes and ears open, talked together of the things we had seen and heard, and each kept a diary of our daily activities and observations. My wife's presence was extremely helpful in this regard, for she saw things that I completely overlooked because of being a man. Further, two viewpoints of the same event revealed insights not otherwise available.

• *Visits.* Our hosts and their friends took us to a variety of places: towns, farms, and places of special interest such as the Taal Volcano. They also saw to it that we were invited to various social events including a baptism, a wedding, and a banquet.

• *Interviews.* Everyone with whom we came into contact became a potential respondent. Sometimes there was no directed conversation; at other times, we specifically asked questions that were designed to increase our information.

• *Survey tools.* Lists of organizations and families were presented to respondents to determine the completeness of the lists and the status rankings of the families.

• *Analysis.* Models of analysis were utilized that enabled us to elicit raw data and from this to develop preliminary hypotheses. These were then refined in keeping with discoveries in the field. Further hypotheses were formed and checked out with our North American and Latin American cultural experiences, as well as from our reading and from our discussions with others.

• *Reading.* A large part of our resource material was found in social anthropological and ethnohistorical reading materials authored by Father Frank Lynch, Mary Hollnsteiner, Fred Eggan, George Guthrie, John Phelan and others (see Bibliography). The quality of this material is, in my estimation, excellent. I had originally anticipated having to discover for myself much of the lifeway, but found that I only had to check the available material for consistency and add this to my own insights.

The material in this study is in no way complete; it serves more as a "pump-primer" rather than as an exhaustive presentation. Significant principles that will aid the North American in the understanding of the Filipino lifeway have been presented and discussed. What use the North

American makes of these principles is up to him, but he would do well to make use of them since these are the principles the Filipino himself uses both in living and in relating to his own people. They are also the principles by which the Filipino will evaluate the worth of the North American in his midst. The North American will find in their application a significant release of conflict and its attendant frustrations. The recommendations are merely suggestive. They simply say, "Look, you don't have to make these Filipinos into North Americans in order to establish satisfactory relationships." If this volume helps to develop such attitudes it will have accomplished its purpose.

Chapter 1

Making Contact with the Filipino

It is a popular misconception to believe that everyone understands what we say and what we do exactly as we intend it to be understood. This simply is not true. We think, act, and speak out of a world and life-view developed within the context of our experiences. For everyone in the world the contexts differ—thus responses to stimuli differ.

In making contact with the Filipino, the North American sincerely desires to communicate effectively and, in turn, to respond correctly. But this is not as easy as we might think. For instance, Americans use idioms that to them are friendly, cute, playful, and designed to gain rapport with others. They will say to their children, "You eat like a pig," as a corrective jest. The Filipino hearing this is affronted; to him it is a serious rebuke.

On the other hand, the Filipino will greet an American with, "You are looking good and fat." To him a fat belly is the sign of success, progress, and wealth. But the American is insulted; to him being fat indicates lack of attention to significant aspects of his manliness. And so the interaction of American with Filipino is frought with pitfalls. Many of these are unknown and unrecognizable by the average person, so the chances of undermining the trust relationship between the two are many.

The following examples are situations which will demonstrate some of these misunderstandings. First we will consider the Filipino responses to the American, and then the American responses to the Filipino.

FILIPINO RESPONSES

SITUATION 1: An American sees a cute little Filipino child and exclaims, "Isn't he a cute little monkey!"
American intent: He is a cute child.

Filipino response: The American thinks my child is just a crude animal.

SITUATION 2: An American sees a Filipino and says, "Hi! How are you?"
American intent: Extending a greeting and showing interest, but not needing extensive response.
Filipino response: The American is two-faced, superficial, and has no real interest unless he listens to an explanation of how I am.

SITUATION 3: An American is enthused that a Filipino is going to have a baby.
American intent: Showing sincere interest in the people.
Filipino response: The American wants to be a godparent of my baby. That's good!

SITUATION 4: The American greets his wife in public with a kiss, a natural response to him.
American intent: To express his love and consideration to his wife.
Filipino response: A vulgar display, something that a well-bred person would refrain from doing in public.

SITUATION 5: An American man smiles in a friendly way at a Filipino woman.
American intent: To be friendly and nice.
Filipino response: He likes me in a special (sexual) way.

SITUATION 6: An American man, perhaps a professor or Sunday School teacher, maintains eye contact with a Filipino woman for a time length normal to him—thirty to fifty seconds.
American intent: To show friendly concern and to pique the woman's interest in the subject.
Filipino response: He sees straight through me. He makes me feel naked.

SITUATION 7: An American woman goes to the beach wearing a bikini but has no robe to cover herself.
American intent: To get a tan.
Filipino response: A cheap, vulgar display showing lack of taste or careful upbringing.

SITUATION 8: An American couple is seen together holding hands.
American intent: Whether they are engaged or not, they like each other.
Filipino response: They are engaged.

SITUATION 9: An American woman goes out in public in a sleeveless dress.

American intent: To be comfortable in the hot humid weather of the Philippines.
Filipino response: Such lack of taste!

Americans also have personal and hygienic habits that Filipinos consider as vulgar, repulsive and unnatural. For example, the American man considers that a healthy, outdoor body odor signifies manliness, but this odor is offensive to the Filipino. An American may clear his throat and either swallow the phlegm or spit it into his handkerchief if he is not outdoors. This is unsanitary and repulsive to the Filipino who feels it should be eliminated wherever one is. The American will generally try to have a flush toilet, even in rural areas. The Filipino thinks this is unnecessary and unnatural, especially for the rural area.

This type of unexpected and, to the American, uncalled-for response extends even into the church. The schedule-conscious American cannot understand why the Filipino has little interest in preparing or following a bulletin. When he enters the average small church, he is disturbed that there is no usher to direct him to a seat. If he knew to look for the pastor's wife, however, she would direct him to an empty seat. Of course, the American would immediately ask, "Why should the pastor's wife have to direct the seating?" The answer is that, in such a situation, the Filipino pastor's wife takes the place of the usher. She feels that it is her place to do it, and in fact, she enjoys doing it.

However, it is not only the Filipino who is mis-cued. The American responding to stimuli provided by the Filipino falls into the same trap. The American, as a visitor in the Filipino society, has much to learn.

The following situations reveal typical American responses to the Filipino situations.

AMERICAN RESPONSES

SITUATION 1: A Filipino man talking with an American man may hold his hand.
Filipino intent: To show acceptance, friendliness, and respect.
American response: This guy is sick. What is the matter with him?
Comment: The Filipino is far more a "touch" person than the American. The only time an American man will touch the body of another man is when they are shaking hands or engaged in some sports activity. The Filipino man will touch another member of the same sex by holding hands, placing an arm around his shoulder, or resting a hand on the leg. None of these are "sex signals" to the Filipino; they are instead signs to show friendliness, trust, acceptance, assurance, and respect.

7

SITUATION 2: The Filipino will belch after a meal.
Filipino intent: To show appreciation for the food. The better the food, the more intense the belch.
American response: A vulgar habit that has no place at the table.
Comment: The Filipino has numerous eating habits and responses which include everything from what he eats and how he eats it to how he shows his appreciation for it. The Filipino uses his fingers for more than fried chicken. He will refuse a beverage until the end of the meal, or he will not eat solids if they are served after a beverage. A Filipino hostess serves cold fish and other delicacies which are unappetizing to some Americans. At a banquet, the hot food may be placed on the table long before it can be eaten and it gets cold, because a high status person has not yet arrived. An American likes his food hot. In fact, the preparation and service of food is so important to him that he may become indignant if it is served cold when it should be hot, a situation that does not bother the average Filipino.

SITUATION 3: The Filipino policeman will blow the whistle at an American.
Filipino intent: To keep traffic moving.
American response: He wants my attention, I had better stop.

SITUATION 4: An American driving in traffic may hear a horn honked behind him.
Filipino intent: To warn the driver, "Stay where you are. I have the right of way in passing you, having honked before you got too far out in the other lane."
American response: I had better get out of his way. So he does, much to the chagrin of the Filipino.
Comment: Obviously, the Filipino has a distinct set of signals involving sound, body movement, and vision that are unlike those of the American. In addition to the above situations, the Filipino points with his lips—a vulgar practice to the American's way of thinking. He also waves good-bye with his fingers turned upward (the Spanish form), which signals "come here" to the American. The reverse signal (fingers down) is also confusing to the American for it signals "come here" to the Filipino, but "good-bye" to the American. The flat of the hand turned outward, away from the body, is a warning signal to the Filipino, but is simply a waving pattern to the American. A Filipino raises his eyebrows to indicate assent, but this body movement is totally overlooked by the American who expects a verbal response. A hand stuck out of the right-hand window of a car to signal a right turn

8

completely frustrates the American who thinks the person is waving to a friend rather than signaling a direction. The American signals only out of the left window.

SITUATION 5: The Filipino family members may dress and undress in front of other members of the family.

Filipino intent: A normal, healthy procedure with no sexual overtones whatsoever.

American response: Provocative and in poor taste. It is offensive to the American who provides a private place for every member of his family for these purposes.

Comment: The American sees the Filipino's practices of dressing and undressing quite differently from what is intended. The Filipino will walk outside in his pajamas with no robe, and the child may run around with no pants on. Sandals are regarded as slippers by the Filipino woman, and are not worn in public by people with good taste.

SITUATION 6: When an employer vocally reprimands his Filipino employee, the Filipino remains silent.

Filipino intent: To show respect.

American response: Uncalled-for insolence.

Comment: There is possibly nothing more infuriating to the American than the response of silence, for he expects a vocal response to his vocal rebuke. Yet the Filipino will remain silent when he wants to show respect, when he wishes to cool an argument, or when he is hurt by another.

SITUATION 7: A Filipino woman returning from the hairdresser will be teased by her friends who say, "How will you preserve that tonight?"

Filipino intent: Responsible, friendly teasing about her plans to make love with her husband that night.

American response: How vulgar and distasteful.

SITUATION 8: A Filipino man may excuse himself from a group by saying, "Excuse me, I have to urinate."

Filipino intent: A responsible excuse understood by all.

American response: What a vulgar statement! He should know better as a grown man.

Comment: In other words, many things that are vulgar and even obscene to an American are everyday matters to a Filipino. The reverse is just as true.

SITUATION 9: The Filipino woman, who has darker skin coloring than the American, will use an umbrella to protect herself from the sun.

Filipino intent: To keep her skin from getting darker.
American response: A vain, stupid practice since they have dark skin anyway.

SITUATION 10: A Filipino who receives a Philippine gift item rather than one from the States is disappointed.
Filipino intent: Stateside items are like Marshall Field gifts to the Filipino. (Marshall Field Department store is the most prestigious in the Chicago area.)
American response: They are "uppity" and status seeking.

The following examples show other distinctive differences in what is highly valued in the respective cultures. A bus driver will have beautifully manicured nails. A professional man will always insist on the use of his title. A student will be in school simply to get a better job, rather than to learn. A man will want to play ping-pong rather than go to a football or baseball game.

These values, which are built into the Filipino system and draw out the natural response of the people, are seen as childish, useless, or unfortunate by the American who has different values.

There are a number of other examples of cultural differences that can be mentioned here. A Filipino may borrow money and return it with goods or services, rather than with money plus interest, as the American expects. The Filipino may borrow tools from the American and loan them to his friends thus delaying their return. The original owner may even have to collect them. The Filipino may wear his wedding band on his right hand. The American may think he is widowed or seeking to mislead people into thinking he is unmarried. A Filipino will hold a wake for a person who has died, which the American considers morbid.

Contact with the Filipino, even as with anyone else, involves responding to the lifeway of his society in keeping with the value orientation of that society. The Filipino has a distinctive lifeway that is not only valid, but rich in past development and in present expression. The following chapters open the larger culture to the reader's comprehension and place the situations of first encounter in a larger perspective.

Chapter 2

The Family

The Filipino society may be broadly characterized as centered in the family and rooted in the soil. It is a young, literate, Roman Catholic nation with an increasing national unity. Although basically homogeneous in culture, it is heterogeneous in local languages and loyalties.

Geography has made the Philippines an Asian country, but history has made it a unique blend of the East and West. By selecting patterns from both East and West, a structure has emerged which is uniquely Filipino.

The general characteristics of Filipino culture and society stem from three basic strands in their social fabric—family, religion, and land. The family is the basic social unit of Filipino society. From it radiate all areas of activities.

The unit of personal involvement with Filipino society centers on the individual (ego) in relationship to his immediate kin and extends out to a network of reciprocal obligations.[1]

The conventional kinship system[2] includes the nuclear (primary or elementary) family composed of a husband (father), his wife (mother), and their children in a union recognized by the society.

Depth of generation through extension of the family

The degree of relationship which ego has with his kin is determined by the generational depth of his relation to the kin group in the ascending generations.

The following diagram by F. Landa Jocano illustrates the structural framework of collateral kin of any generation to the one immediately above it[3] (see figure 1a).

The Filipino kinship system can also be extended bilaterally to in-

11

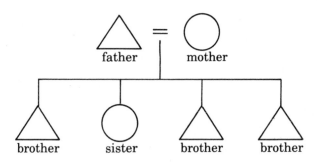

Figure 1a. **Collateral Kin**

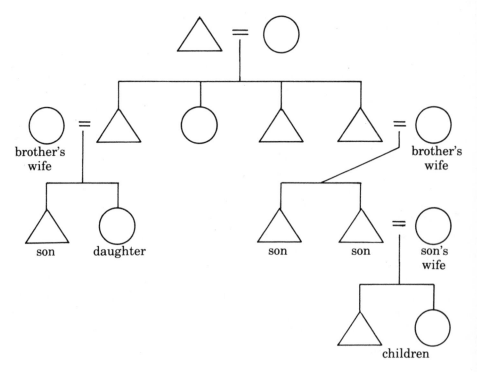

Figure 1b. **Bilateral Extension**

clude an almost indefinite range of relatives, but actual consanguinity is only recognized in one's third (sometimes fourth) cousins on either the father's or the mother's side (see figure 1b).

The generational-bilateral kinship system is organized on the principle of generation. One's kin of each generation are clearly defined and differentiated by a distinct set of referential and vocative kinship terms. Lineal relatives are set off from collateral relatives in every generation.

Extension of the family by marriage

Through marriage two kinship groups are linked together. Affinal kin, or in-laws, add to the kinship grouping, for the spouse's relationships become his as well. In the Philippines, one marries a family, not just a fiancé.[4]

The marriage process involves a sequence of preparations similar to those in North American society in that there is a period of dating, an engagement, and a wedding. The difference between the two societies lies in subtle distinctions of expected behavior patterns, the period of time that the process consumes and the implications of progress through the various stages of preparation.

When a young man has decided that he likes a girl and would like to marry her (not just casually date her as in the States), he sends a number of messages to her. Her answers to these messages are designed to inform him if she is interested in him, or if he should look for someone else. First, he will look at the girl in a special way, telling her without words that he is interested. Next, he may also inform another person who is normally close to the girl. This intermediary is expected to drop hints to the girl that a certain friend is interested in her. It has been said that the way to a girl's heart is through her best friend.

When these preliminary steps have been taken and the girl is interested, she will say something like, "Well, why doesn't he say so?" This attitude is reported to the interested party and he understands that she is interested in him. So he will write a letter to the girl informing her of his interest. If the letter is not responded to, he will send her flowers. The next time they are together, he will ask her for a reply to his letter. The girl probably will not reply at this time, but instead will play it cool. Then the boy will follow up with a request that he go to her home to meet her family. She will not give a direct reply but will say "Maybe," or "If you would like to." She would never say yes even if her response was yes. But her indirect responses are sufficient to encourage the fellow to call at her home. In case the girl has strict parents, an alternative possibility would be indirectly suggested and the two would meet in a restaurant, a park or some other public spot where their meeting would appear to be by chance.[5] The early dating period in Filipino society takes less time in comparison to the North American practice, but is also more limited in possible activities.

Once the girl has indicated her willingness to date the young man, they both prepare for the visitation period. This becomes the courtship, or the equivalent of the North American "going steady;" however, it is much more serious. By now, the intent is marriage for the Filipino couple whereas in the United States, dating may show only friendship. Although it is still a possibility, marriage as a goal is not as clearly spelled out for the American youth. The Filipino calls this period "going up to court someone," or "up a staircase." The implication is that he is courting his girl.

Although the girl personally likes the fellow, she cannot be totally committed to him until he gets her parents' approval. Therefore, the young man now actively engages in sending feelers to see if the girl's family likes him. He will take gifts to his girl and to her family as well, for he knows he is being carefully scrutinized, and he wants to make the best possible impression. Immediately following his visit, the entire family will evaluate the young man in the girl's presence with either praise or criticism. Many times this provides fun and entertainment for the family, especially if the young man has peculiar characteristics.

If the family does not approve but the girl is still interested, she will carefully conceal her emotions at home and continue seeing the fellow elsewhere. As a result, the family will not know when she finally commits herself to her suitor—something they would know immediately had they given their approval. The couple will work hard to change the family attitude. If unsuccessful, they may resolve the problem either by eloping or by breaking up.

During this entire period of courtship, which may last for a number of years, the couple will not hold hands, kiss, or show endearments by physical contact. Even after she has committed herself to him, they will not hold hands in front of their parents. Such contact is reserved for when they are in school or at the movies.

When the relationship has become serious, the fellow, after consulting with his girl and his own parents, will go to the girl's parents and ask for her hand in marriage.[6] Then the young man and his parents will go together to the parents of the girl and formally arrange for the ceremony.

In this meeting between both sets of parents, every tradition followed by either family will be discussed and included in the wedding plans. An example of such tradition would be that the wedding day cannot be Friday, or the moon cannot be in a certain phase. If there is a conflict of family traditions, a compromise is worked out.[7]

Extension of the family by taking a mistress

A husband may have extra-marital relations without being censured by anyone. He may go night-clubbing with a girl friend, maintain a steady girl friend, or have a common-law wife. However, his legal wife is condemned if she goes out with another man. It is accepted that a man retains his natural physical powers no matter what he does, but a woman, because she may become pregnant, does not retain her powers. She changes physically. Virtue and purity is expected of a woman, especially virginity before marriage. Though a man always wants to be a woman's first lover, the woman hopes that she will be his last.

Although the married woman will take great precautions to keep her husband from "running around," eventually he will likely slip away from her. After unsuccessfully doing all she can to stop his excursions, she will ultimately resign herself to the situation. Her friends will then try to console her with statements such as, "After all, you are number one," or "As long as he gives you his full salary, it is all right," and "The procession, no matter where it reaches, will return to the church just the same," or more pointedly, "The husband, wherever he would roam, must always return home."

Extension of the family ritually

The ritual extension of kinship is known as the system of *compadrazgo*. It was originally introduced into the Philippines as a part of the Roman Catholic heritage and was intended by the church authorities to ensure that the child would be educated in the faith. Since then, it has become part of the Filipino culture and has taken on a broader significance than simply perpetuating church doctrine.

Robert S. Fox discusses the organization and function of the *compadre* system. He says,

> The basic organization principle . . . *compadrazgo* . . . functions to systematize and normatize relationships between unrelated individuals (families) based upon . . . kinship. The socially and emotionally secure relationships of kinship are reduplicated and extended by *compadrazgo*, a function of considerable importance in view of the potential conflict underlying all interpersonal relationships between nonkinsmen, a result of the Filipino's concept of "self-esteem" or *hiya*. . . . *Compadrazgo* provides a means of ordering hierarchical relations (landlord-tenant, employer-employee, high-low status), a channel for upward mobility and possibly a mechanism of out-migration from the rural to urban areas.[8]

This larger kin group, or *compadrazgo*, is formed through the rituals of baptism, confirmation, and marriage. The nonkindred sponsors for these occasions become linked to the family and are expected to help the family, but they may also expect to be helped by the family when the occasion arises. This helping relationship is known as reciprocal rights and obligations, or *utang na loob*. The effect of the ritual relationship is to make the ritual relative as if he were family.

With the performance of baptism, confirmation, or marriage, three additional sets of group relationship with nonkinsmen develop for the child and his family.[9]

Coparents not only help the family to which they are linked but they also help each other. Godparents are interested in and often help with the rearing and education of a godchild. In return, the godchild helps the godparent when such help is needed. The relationship is the same as between parent and child.

Perhaps the key point of contact between the godparent and the godchild is at Christmas. Here the relationship is reinforced as the godparent presents the godchild with a gift. If the godchild is an infant, he takes the gift to the child's home. But when the child is old enough to claim the gift, he must go to the godparent's home. This practice ceases when the child reaches a mature age, but while it is in operation, it serves as a seal of the original contract and the pledge of future assistance. When the child reaches maturity, the provision of a job, a year's tuition at a university, or some other form of assistance or favor substitutes for the yearly gift.

The ritual kinship extends the family to include two or more nuclear families making them economically and socially related to each other. Through this extension of the family, an alliance nucleus is developed. The alliance nucleus is the group of friends that are brought one by one into a symbolic family relationship to ego through the practice of ritual kinship (see figure 2).

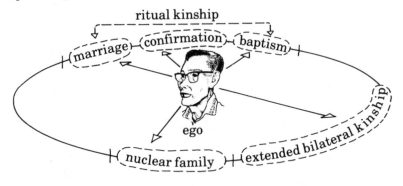

Figure 2. **The Alliance Nucleus**

Notes and references

[1] For instance, see F. Landa Jocano. *Growing up in a Philippine Barrio.* Holt, Rinehart, and Winston, New York, 1969, 75–82.

[2] For background discussion of kinship systems in general see:

Fred Eggan. "Kinship; Introduction." *International Encyclopedia of the Social Sciences.* Vol. 8, 390–401.

John Freeman. "The Concept of Kindred." *Journal of the Royal Anthropological Institute.* Vol. 91, No. 2, July-December, 1961, 192–220.

A. R. Radcliffe-Brown. "The Study of Kinship Systems," in *Structure and Function in Primitive Society.* The Free Press, New York, 1952.

Ernest L. Schusky. *Manual for Kinship Analysis.* Studies in Anthropological Method Series, Holt, Rinehart and Winston, New York, 1965. This is a helpful little handbook.

[3] F. Landa Jocano. *Sulod Society.* University of Philippines Press, Manila, 1968, 67.

[4] For additional study of Filipino kinship systems in particular see:

Roy F. Barton. *Ifugao Law.* University of California Press, Berkeley, 1969. This is one of the earliest studies to contribute to our understanding of bilateral social systems. Barton also realized that "kinship circles" are the basis for social relationships among the Ifugaos.

Edward P. Dozier. "Social Organization and Social Life," in *The Kalinga of Northern Luzon, Philippines.* Holt, Rinehart and Winston, New York, 1967.

Ronald S. Himes. "The Bontoc Kinship System." *Philippine Sociological Review.* Vol. 12, 1964, 159–172.

F. Landa Jocano. *Sulod Society: A Study in Kinship System and Social Organization of a Mountain People of Central Pandy.* University of the Philippines Press, Quezon City, 1968.

Alfred Louis Kroeber. "Kinship in the Philippines." *Anthropological Papers of the American Museum of Natural History.* Vol. 14, No. 3, 1919, 69–84.

[5] Generally parents want the fellow to come and see their daughter in their home instead of meeting her in the street. It is considered poor taste if he does not visit her at home.

[6] This is called *mamamanhikan* from the root word *panhik*, or "go up the stairs."

[7] For additional information on marriage and the family in the Philippines, see the following sources:

Noli de los Angeles. "Marriage and Fertility Patterns in the Philippines." *Philippine Sociological Review.* Vol. 13, No. 4, October, 1965, 232–248.

John Carroll. *Changing Patterns of Social Structure in the Philippines, 1896–1963.* Ateneo de Manila University Press, Quezon City, 1968, 34–36, 134–140.

Felicidad V. Cordero and Isabel S. Panopio. *General Sociology: Focus on the Philippines.* College Professors Publishing Corporation, Manila, 1968, especially chapters 13 and 14.

Ruben Santos Cuyugan. "Socio-Cultural Change and the Filipino Family." *Science Review*. Vol. 2, No. 3, March, 1961, 203–205.

Robert B. Fox. "The Family and Society in the Rural Philippines." *Science Review*. National Science Development Board, Manila, April, 1961, 1–5.

———. "The Filipino Family in Perspective," in *Saturday Parade Magazine*, The Evening News, Manila, October 15, 1960.

Frank Lynch. "The Conjugal Bond where the Philippines Changes." *Philippine Sociological Review*. Vol. 7, No. 3–4, July-October, 1960, 48–51.

Alfredo G. Pacyaya. "Changing Customs of Marriage, Death, and Burial among the Sagada Igorots." *Practical Anthropology*. Vol. 8, 1961, 125–133.

Julius W. Pratt. "Family Size and Expectations in Manila." *Saint Louis Quarterly*. Vol. 5, No. 1–2, 153–184.

Lourdes Quisumbing. "Characteristic Features of the Cebuano Family Life." *Philippine Sociological Review*. Vol. 11, No. 1–2, January-April, 1963, 135–141.

Harriet R. Reynolds. "The Filipino Family in its Cultural Setting." *Practical Anthropology*. Vol. 9, 1962, 223–234.

Daniel J. Scheans. "The Ilocano: Marriage and the Land." *Philippine Sociological Review*. Vol. 13, No. 1, January, 1965, 57–62.

[8] Robert B. Fox. "Social Organization." *Human Relations Area File*, Vol. 1, Philippines (Chicago: University of Chicago, n.d.), 1956, 429–430.

[9] For further discussion of *compadrazgo*, see:

George M. Foster. "*Confradia* and *Compadrazgo* in Spain and Spanish America." *Southwestern Journal of Anthropology*. Vol. 9, 1953, 10ff.

Robert B. Fox and Frank Lynch. "Social Organization; Ritual Coparenthood." *Area Handbook on the Philippines*. Supervising editors, Fred Eggan and others. The University of Chicago for Human Relations Area Files, 1956, Vol. 1, 424–430.

Mary R. Hollnsteiner. *The Dynamics of Power in a Philippine Municipality*. Community Development Research Council, University of the Philippines, Quezon City, 1963, 64–65, 69–71.

Sidney W. Mintz and Eric R. Wolf. "An Analysis of Ritual Coparenthood (*Compadrazgo*)," *Southwestern Journal of Anthropology*. Vol. 6, 1950 341–368.

Chapter 3

The Alliance

The alliance as a structured unit

The alliance is perhaps the most significant unit of the social struc-ture operating in the Filipino society. It fulfills various functions within the larger society, such as providing the basic pattern for friendship, protecting personal possessions, and providing the major socialization of the children. It also forms the economic base of support since it is the primary source of capital and loan funds.

The core of the alliance (see figure 3) is consanguineal, in that blood relatives form the immediate associating group that becomes the alliance;

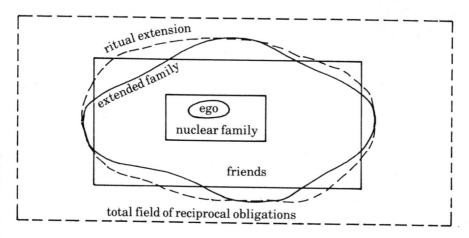

Figure 3. **The Alliance**

however, the membership of the alliance is never fixed. The ritual extension of the alliance through the godparent relationship keeps the alliance expanding and growing. People who become meaningful in some way are invited to become part of it as godparents. **If someone enters an alliance by means of the ritual extension route, he becomes "somebody." If he never becomes a godparent, he will be a "nobody."**[1]

The primary socialization of children is carried out in the alliance and is their most important education. Through it the child learns his basic lessons of interpersonal relationships as well as how to perceive the world beyond. A discontinuity exists between his school education and his primary socialization. Because of this, very little of what the average Filipino child learns in school will seriously alter the training provided by the alliance. School education is learned as an entirely different system of knowledge and it has little relevance to his everyday experiences.

Above all else, ego's primary loyalties are to the members of his alliance. If there is anything of real, enduring worth, the Filipino expects that it will find expression within the alliance. If someone is important, his importance will be verified, or even realized, through the alliance. **If someone hopes to achieve a loyalty response to a person or program, he must work in some way through the alliance.**

Each alliance is ranked—thus tied into the status system—and has its corporate standing within the whole society in keeping with its rank. Every individual also has his place within the status system in keeping with his ranking within his own alliance. Status controls the behavior and influence of the individual as well as the group. Every alliance fits into a complex system of interpersonal and intergroup relationships which makes up the fabric of Filipino society. **Unless someone is associated with an alliance, his place in society is ambiguous and must be constantly clarified.** This consumes much of the energy of the contact.

All alliances have a leader or a head. The leader will always have the highest status. If an alliance has only members of one extended family, then the father is the leader with the highest prestige. If a number of friends are in an alliance, the friend with the highest status is looked to for final decision in leadership. The leader is responsible for the well-being of the entire alliance, and all lines of authority trace ultimately to that person, whether male or female. The leader can be either male or female since lineage is traced bilaterally in Filipino society. Males, however, predominate as recognized leaders. **There is no request im-**

possible to fulfill when the head of an alliance is on one's side and obligated to one within the pattern of reciprocal obligation.

The individual is of the highest value in the Philippines. He can, ultimately, do what he wants to do even though his actions may upset others. Also, although the most effective route of personal fulfillment is through loyalty to the alliance, nevertheless the society affirms, and reaffirms, his individual rights. Outsiders are scandalized by this ego assertion and assume it will be punished, but the Filipino knows that this is his ultimate prerogative. The alliance, not the nation, is the dominant value group within the total society.[2] In North America the individual is unable to act contrary to the will of the nation,[3] but the Filipino nation is unable to act contrary to the sum total of the will of the alliance. In other words, the alliance is always placed above all other interests, including national interests, except in situations when the individual perceives the will of the alliance as being contrary to his own. In that case, the individual comes first.

Members of alliances, as well as alliances, are tied together through the practice of mutual reciprocity, *utang na loob*. When a person reciprocates with another, he becomes a "somebody" in society as a member of an alliance. If there is a lack of reciprocity, the offending person is slowly eased out of association with the alliance and, consequently, with the society. Patterns of reciprocity bind alliances and society together into a complex functioning whole. **The base of power in the Filipino nation is the individual defending or living by his *amor propio*, (self-love) and so controlling the alliance.**

Ego's loyalty and the alliance

Ego's loyalties to the alliance come before his loyalties to his nation, a stranger,[4] or to a North American acquaintance. Because the North American misunderstands the Filipino's loyalty priorities, he tends to react with anger when the Filipino appears to break his word, i.e., changing a previous commitment after encountering a member of his alliance.

One characteristic situation is for a Filipino maid to entertain other Filipinos in the North American's home while they are away, even though she was instructed to the contrary. Although the maid sincerely desires and intends to heed the North American's request, yet, when her cousins, *kinakapatid* (children of her godparents), or other alliance members come to the house, her first loyalty is to them. If they invite themselves to sleep overnight and take the liberty of sleeping in the master's bed, the Filipino maid cannot stop them. Her loyalty to the

21

alliance pressures her to cater to their desires. She can afford to lose her job, but she dare not prejudice her relationship with the alliance.

In another situation, a Filipino church elder will agree with a missionary as to how things should be done. The missionary, assured of the elder's support, will confidently attend the church board meeting. But imagine his bitter disappointment when he finds out that the elder completely reversed his stand and voted against him. "The Filipino is a weakling or a traitor," he accuses. But, actually, the elder is just putting his loyalty to the alliance first. His decision must follow the will of his alliance if two-thirds of the board members happen to belong to his alliance.

Loyalty to the alliance is further illustrated when one member receives a large sum of money, or wins a lottery. Investment of this money is very rare, and happens only in cases where something is left after handouts are made to relatives and close friends. If an individual wins a lottery, he must share his good fortune with others. The one who doesn't share is frowned upon, considered greedy and selfish, and ostracized. Many common Filipino expressions reinforce this belief; for example, "by the pity or grace of God," and "just by luck."

Occasions for giving cash handouts to friends and relatives may occur after winning a bet in a cockfight, at mahjong, at the races, and in the sweepstakes or lottery. However, when a person gets a big increase in salary, gets a job promotion, is elected to some position, or passes the bar or board examination, there will be an elaborate party rather than cash handouts. Friends and relatives not only expect such behavior from the winner, but often remind him of his obligation.

Usually, the winner is happy to share his winnings. One woman doctor, after winning the lottery, was advised by North Americans to invest the money for her future. But the doctor responded with great depth of feeling, "Were I to do that, I couldn't sleep at night."

The dependency factor in alliance relationships

A child is never left alone in a room; someone is always with him. In the provinces and barrios, children sleep with the parents. This is partly necessitated by the need to sleep under a mosquito net, and group sleeping cuts down the need for more than one net. Because of this custom, however, the child becomes afraid to sleep alone. Even as teenagers or adults, they share the mosquito net with brothers, sisters, and other relatives. When sent on an errand, a child will seek out a younger brother, sister, or friend to accompany him.

This practice continues into the courtship period. A companion or chaperone usually accompanies the girl on a date. This practice is perpetuated as much by the girl as by her parents.[5] The chaperone may be a good friend, a relative, or a younger brother or sister sent by the mother to watch that the couple behaves. Even when going to the market, to church or to shop, the girl will take a companion for moral support, intermediary service, or safety.

The guest in the Filipino home is never left alone. There is always a maid or a family member nearby; or the lights are turned on in the guest's immediate vicinity. This is a courtesy extended by the Filipino, and it is in keeping with his sense of responsibility for the well-being of the guest. The North American reacts adversely to such a practice. He feels he can never be alone. At times he wishes to read, meditate, or plan, but he must go to his room and shut the door to find the privacy to do so. If he is relaxing in a more public area of the house, someone will be there to keep him company. At other times, the North American wants to enjoy a few quiet moments on the patio in the moonlight or under the brilliant stars; but within seconds of his entering the patio, the lights will be turned on.

Filipinos are also dependent in decision making. It usually involves two to make a decision—the person who must ultimately make up his mind, and his companion. In large decisions, or small, the decision-making process is shared; i.e., what course of action to follow, which girl to court, which suitor to entertain, etc. The Filipino relies upon the majority of the family, or upon his companion, to decide for him. In this way he is freed from responsibility—not to be irresponsible—but to be responsible in a corporate, not individual, sense. The Filipino depends upon others.

The North American reacts strongly to this practice. It strikes him as abandoning responsibility and as being unable to make up his mind. Questions such as, "Can't you make up your own mind?" "Can't you decide things for yourself?" flood the mind of the North American.

When asked by a North American why she married the man preferred by her parents, and not the man she loved, the Filipino answered, "So that if we have a bad marriage, it will not be my fault. My parents will be the ones responsible for it."

Dependency upon parents continues even after marriage and the birth of children.[6] When the couple tries to live by themselves, or to run their own lives, others wonder, "Are they not on good terms with the old folks?" Or, "The parents have such bad *ugali* (customs, manners, or habits) that even their own children don't want to stay with them." Thus independence reflects upon both the couple and the parents. But when a family stays together and makes decisions together, they evoke a picture of happiness and good relationships.

Notes and references

[1] The alliance system and ritual extension of the alliance is also discussed by Mary R. Hollnsteiner in *The Dynamics of Power in a Philippine Municipality*. Community Development Research Council, University of the Philippines, Quezon City, 1963, 63–71, 77–78, 91.

The concept of "nobody" is also illustrated by the Filipino's reluctance to offer help, give directions or any form of aid to a stranger. Yet, he does not hesitate to get involved if he knows the other person. (This reluctance is also directly related to the Filipino's basic values. See chapter 13.)

[2] For further study, see also:

Frank Lynch. *Social Class in a Bikol Town*. University of Chicago, Chicago, 1959, 49–55.

John J. Carroll. *Changing Patterns of Social Structure in the Philippines, 1896–1963*. Ateneo de Manila University Press, Quezon City, 1968, 188.

Vitaliano R. Gorospe. "Christian Renewal of Filipino Values," in *Split-Level Christianity (and) Christian Renewal of Philipino Values*. Ateneo University Press, Quezon City, 1966, 19–59.

[3] This is especially true of some middle class American subcultures. A man goes to war to make the world safe for democracy, even though his family needs him; he attends church or business functions though he may want to be with his children; and he takes a walk with his children though he wants to work on a hobby.

[4] The person we consider a stranger, the Filipino tends to see as a potential alliance member. It is only when there does not seem to be any possibility of forming an alliance relationship or after an alliance relationship has been rejected that a person becomes a stranger.

[5] It is not unusual for a Filipino girl residing in the United States to have her first unchaperoned date with a North American fellow. Often this is resisted and numerous dates are turned down until the girl gets up the nerve to accept.

[6] For further study on child rearing in the Philippines, see the section on multialternatives in chapter 13 of this text as well as the following publications:

Nena B. Eslao. "Child Rearing Among the Samals of Manubul, Siasi, Sulu," *Philippine Sociological Review*. Vol. 10, No. 3–4, July-October, 1962, 80–91.

George M. Guthrie. *The Filipino Child and Philippine Society*. Philippine Normal College Press, Manila, 1961.

—— and Pepita Jimenez Jacobs. *Child Rearing and Personality Development in the Philippines*. The Pennsylvania State University Press, University Park, Pennsylvania, 1966.

Rachel Hare. "Cultural Differences in the Use of Guilt and Shame in Child Rearing: A Review of the Research on the Philippines and Other non-Western Societies," in *Modernization: Its Impact in the Philippines II*. Ateneo de Manila University Press, Quezon City, 1967, 35–76.

F. Landa Jocano. *Growing up in a Philippine Barrio*. Holt, Rinehart, and Winston, New York, 1969.

Ethel Nurge. "Economic Functions of the Child in the Rural Philippines." *Philippine Sociological Review*. Vol. 4, No. 1, January 1956, 7–11.

———. *Life in a Leyte Village*. University of Washington Press, Seattle, 1965.

William F. Nydegger and Corinne Nydegger. *Tarong: An Ilocos Barrio in the Philippines*. Six Culture Series: Vol. 6. John Wiley and Sons, New York, 1966.

Beatrice Whiting, Ed. *Six Cultures: Studies on Child Rearing*. John Wiley and Sons, New York, 1963.

Chapter 4

Linking Alliances

As soon as birth or marriage occurs, the head of the alliance draws together various members of the extended family, i.e., those associating regularly, ritual members, and friends "on the way in." His leadership also draws the group into a basic solidarity which provides security for all of its members. Although the security is in the social realm primarily, it also extends into the economic, religious, and political realms.

Characteristic alliance linkages

The strength of Filipino society rests in the linked alliances (see figure 4) rather than in the individual alliances. The individual alliance is simply the microcosm of the macrocosm. Such linkage of many alliances provides security primarily in the political realm, and the nation

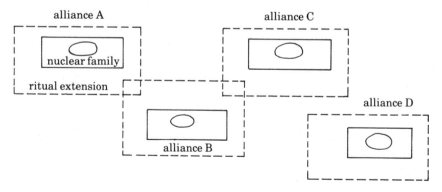

Figure 4. **Interaction Patterns of Alliances**

27

becomes a massive linkage of alliances. In the same way that the most respected head of the alliances becomes the leader of the linked alliances, so the most respected head of the largest number of linked alliances becomes the president of the nation.

Alliances are grouped by two basic contact linkages—at marriage, and through the sponsor relationship. They may also be related if they so choose by contact with the personality figure (referred to below) who relates to each alliance separately. Alliances may relate through friendship or mutual need, or through patterns of relationship which ultimately produce a linkage through sponsorship at marriage or at the birth of a child.

Contact linkages

Contact linkage of alliances is the most informal one but it produces a strong base for further relationships to develop. Probably the most enduring and important of the contact linkages is that effected by marriage. Members of two alliances marry and this brings them together in a relationship that is new, or that reinforces some former contact. Thereafter, these two alliances will be favorably disposed toward one another in a new way. Although they do not have to become associating groups, they will be open to mutual influence. Alliances previously linked affinally become desirable groups from which to select other marriage partners.

Godparents, or sponsors, are another significant linkage between two alliances. Those sharing the same sponsor will relate in terms of mutual loyalty, though this bond will not be as strong or enduring as the affinal bond. Since most families have an average of six to eight children, and each child has from two to six pairs of sponsors at birth and two to four at marriage, it is easy to conceptualize the total society becoming linked through the ritual relationship. The value of the sponsor relationship is that it produces a favorable climate for marriage. This in turn reinforces the social bond and the directed influence of the personality figure. A favorable relationship to a member of an alliance insures the careful consideration of his request and concern, even if it does not guarantee a favorable response.

A third type of contact linkage is that of friendship. Any friendship will create a loosely formed linkage that will be reinforced in time by the marriage or coparent linkage. It can produce an influence by itself, however, for a couple of years. It only becomes ineffective if there is a refusal to enter more fully into the life of the alliance through the ritual ties at birth or marriage.[1]

28

The personality figure

The personality figure[2] is a personable individual who has some need for influence-support, who can relate to any alliance in terms of their need, and who can especially communicate to them that they are the sole focus of his interest. This may be no more than a perception, but it allows the alliance and the personality figure to have a mutual relationship. It provides the alliance with need fulfillment, and the personality figure with support in his drive for influence-power.

Being personable means that the individual has the ability to project himself as being of higher status than the alliance heads (though this may not actually be the case), has a friendly quality that communicates his sole interest in the alliance, and has the perceived ability to fulfill needs felt by the alliance.

The alliances thus linked by the personality figure do not have to associate in the way that components of the alliance itself associate. The latter is an actual association in a social, economic, religious, or political setting. The former is a potential for relatedness rather than any association. Their identification is with the leader whether they, as alliances, actually do anything together or not.

In the religious domain, Catholic-type involvement is more amenable to the Filipino social structure than the Protestant. The Catholic ritual permits many people to interact with the priest without associating with each other. Each person is an individual entity in relation to the priest. Each alliance is an individual entity in relation to the priest at specific life crisis rituals, e.g., birth, puberty, marriage, or death.

In the Protestant ritual, however, everyone is together as part of the body. They sing, pray, and worship together. In other words, the Protestant people relate to the pastor and to each other as a group, a body, or a corporate entity rather than remaining separate. This forced association between members, however slight, is more than can be borne by the system, and turns many Filipinos away from Protestantism.[3]

Mutual need

Alliances can relate through mutual need just once or many times. There may be neither contact linkage nor association with a multialliance leader during their time of need fulfillment; but, depending on the duration of the need and the extensiveness of fulfillment demand, their relationship could lead to both. The need which brings them together might be for protection from a local enemy, an economic need, or some social crisis.

The multialliance leader

The *eldest male*, generally seen as the alliance head, also becomes the head of many alliances of an extended family when it becomes too large for the continual association of its members. But the number of alliances linked by the eldest male is limited to the size of the extended family.

The *status male* is the highest status person in several linked alliances. These alliances are linked within the local area by affinal ties, ritual ties, or mutual need. Again, the number of alliances linked in this way, though greater than those relating to the eldest male, are limited by the size and contact of the local area.

The *influence-power seeker* extends the consanguineal and local groups and draws alliances to himself that relate to him in terms of a specific interest, such as a political interest with local, provincial, or national extension. The leader attracts these alliances because they are interested in the issue being raised, or because the leader has been able to fill some need for them. Alliances may realign but that does not usually occur until after the leader dies. The power of this alignment is so great that loyalty directed to the leader probably will not shift. The key to such power lies in the nature of reciprocity and the obligations entailed.[4]

The *woman*, as the grantor of favors, is the primary way to influence the leader. When he dies, she replaces him until the position is filled by someone else. Leaders of linked alliances are only replaced at death. Though there is no one man who succeeds him, there might be a subordinate who has greater potential than anyone else to draw together the loose strands of the linked alliances. At such time a realignment of alliances is almost guaranteed. The woman fills a significant role in seeing that this period of readjustment goes smoothly, and that the successor emerges with the greatest number of the alliances under his influence.

If she is still able to exercise influence, the leader's grandmother is most effective in achieving this smooth readjustment. However, if the grandmother is not capable, then the mother, the wife, or, as a last resort, an older sister may use her influence.

As the grantor of favors, the grandmother, mother, or wife fulfils this role most effectively.[5] This appears to be a characteristic of Far Eastern societies. It was effectively reinforced by the Spanish intrusion, since within Spanish society the woman had a very definitive influence over the head of the extended family. Her influence was so powerful that she could actually accomplish anything that she wanted, even though the orders of the male might legislate against her wishes.[6]

Additional functions of the woman within the authority network of Filipino society include being the news (or tale) bearer and being responsible for running the household. This latter implies holding the purse strings—a power felt far beyond the confines of the household. It also sets up the primary socialization of the children, giving them not only the perception of male power but also the realization of female power. The saying in the Philippines is that "man rules but woman reigns." Any man who falls under the power and authority of the woman, or who lets her control over the money extend too far, is said to be henpecked.

The North American reaction

To the American, the nation is a powerful entity itself and is not responsible to families of the nation. A political leader achieves his position through the aid of friends but is not responsible to them in the final analysis. Thus there is a partial linking of families within a political party with an overall effect of party influence, but nothing like the power of the linked alliances in the Philippines. Besides, no two members of a family have to vote the same. If a party leader gets the support of a family member, there is no guarantee that this influence extends beyond the individual.

The family-alliance orientation of the Philippines is responded to negatively by the American. He sees it as undue family influence. The group solidarity formed through the alliance system is incomprehensible to the American, for he sees it as weakness, and he interprets the derived loyalty as the inability of the Filipino to make up his own mind and to stand on his own two feet.

The woman, as leader replacement, is partially understood by the American, but the woman, as grantor of favors, is incomprehensible. He thinks no woman should ever have that much power. The American male feels uncomfortable approaching a client through a woman. This is seen by him as the weakness of the male and, therefore, of the entire society.

Notes and references

[1] This type of relationship trips up the non-Filipino and, especially, the North American Protestant. The friendship progresses beautifully for a couple of years, seeming to flourish. Then when an opportunity arises to seal the relationship and make it enduring, the outsider backs off for some reason. For example, the Protestant will refuse to be a sponsor of a baby because the practice is perceived to be "Catholic," because he will not always be there, or just because he does not want to. As soon as the outsider backs off from the relationship, the Filipino backs off from him and the friendship begins to terminate.

[2] Mary Hollnsteiner's concept of "personalism" mentioned in her summary of Chapter 6 in *The Dynamics of Power in a Philippine Municipality*, seems to be equivalent to the "personality figure" concept used here.

[3] This may partly explain why members of one Catholic church can come from all status sectors of the society; whereas, members of one Protestant church are from a far more limited sector of the society. They usually come from one or two extended families, or, at best, from one or more alliances which are related by marriage.

[4] See also Chapter 9.

[5] *Utos ni Mrs.* is a term that is used to refer to "by the order of Mrs.—," i.e., "one's wife." Originally it was used to refer to papers as the "power" behind Marcos' administration, or that the President's decisions were colored and influenced, if not controlled, by his "Mrs."

[6] See Marvin K. Mayers. *A Look at Latin American Lifestyles*, S.I.L. Museum of Anthropology Publication 2, Dallas, Texas, 1976, 80–83.

Chapter 5

The Nation

The nation as linked alliances

The United States, as a nation, is formed through linkages of political entities (such as states, political parties, and various influence groups), whereas the Philippine nation is formed through the linkage of alliances. The United States is perceived as a monolithic nation with every diverse part lost within the whole, while the Philippine nation is nothing apart from the consensual process of the linked alliances agreeing to action and seeing it fulfilled—or disagreeing and thus undermining the effect of the corporate body.

The highest status leader of a given alliance becomes the leader of the alliance grouping. The leader of the largest grouping of alliances in effect becomes the political leader of all. The process of becoming president of the nation, therefore, begins long before the political campaign. It starts with the struggle of the family to maintain its status level and to improve its standing where possible. It also lies behind every effort made by an aspiring power-influence person to relate to every possible alliance or alliance linkage in ever widening spheres of influence within the nation. Such a power consolidation is more of a natural process than a struggle. The point is to elicit support by building patterns of reciprocity between alliances and alliance leaders, not to dominate others—a probable interpretation by North Americans. The question is not so much, "Where do the power sources lie?" (who is for whom, etc.), but, "Who knows whom?" What pattern of reciprocity has formed? How intense is one's loyalty to another? These are determined by the details of the reciprocal relationship.[1]

The nation as a language-ethnic group

The Philippines consist of about 7,100 islands and islets which dot the East China Sea between Formosa and Indonesia. Topographically, most of these are hilly and mountainous in the interior, and many are too rocky for habitation. Seventy percent of the total land area lies on two large islands, Luzon and Mindanao.[2] A recent census report places the population of the entire country at forty-two million. There are three major Filipino languages which dominate the three largest geographic zones of the Philippines. They are found among the ethnic group speaking Tagalog in central Luzon, the group speaking Ilocano in northern Luzon, and the Cebuano of the island areas south of Luzon.[3] Perhaps because of its central position and proximity to the commercial centers, especially Manila, the Tagalog group has tended in the past to control major political and social developments within the nation. It might be said that "as Manila goes, so goes the Philippines."

Prior to the second World War, the Spanish culture dominated Filipino life and thought. Much of that influence worked itself into the fabric of the society and still exerts itself. The family and status subsystems of the society still reflect strong Spanish influence, though the Spanish language is not spoken to the extent it was formerly.[4] This, in spite of the fact that the North American culture and thought patterns have been the dominant influence and have had increasing impact since World War II.

The nation as social structure

The nation is made up of language-ethnic groups and ruled by an elected president with a vice-president in the executive branch, and the legislative and judicial systems patterned after those of the United States (see figure 5). The social structure further consists of cities and provinces, municipalities, neighborhoods and households.

Cities and provinces are basically autonomous in their government as far as local jurisdiction is concerned. Cities are structurally like provinces, but are geographically included in provinces. They are also like municipalities (see below) in that they supervise surrounding barrios and have an elected mayor, vice-mayor, and seven councilmen. Provinces are geographic divisions which include under their jurisdiction municipalities and barrios. The province is ruled by an elected governor.

Municipalities have jurisdiction over their own affairs as well as supervision of barrios. They are ranked one to seven according to the amount of income tax paid to the government. Barrios are divided into

34

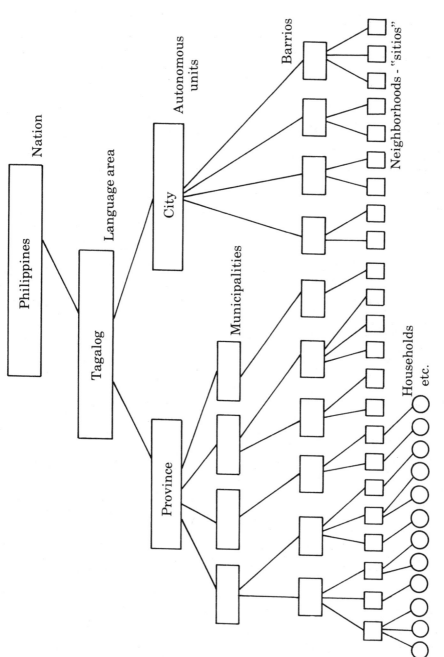

Figure 5. **Social Structure**

conciliar zones, and governed by a captain with lieutenants supervising the various divisions.

Neighborhoods are a loose-knit grouping of households. The neighborhood is usually equivalent to the extended family or alliance.

Households are made up of the nuclear family, household servants, and relatives, the latter being optional.

The North American finds this system compatible with his own nation-state-city-neighborhood-household organization.

The nation as interpenetrating status relationships

The Philippine nation is a complex network of interpersonal and intergroup relationships, founded primarily on the pattern of linked alliances, but it extends from that to groups and persons beyond the alliance operations. These relationships are undergirded by status relationships which, in effect, relate to a given organization, group, or person as higher or lower on the status ladder.

Among the language-ethnic groups, Tagalog is ranked above all other groups. In part, this is due to the historic centrality of Tagalog in the development of the Philippine nation. It is also due partly to geographic location, for the Tagalog occupy the central Luzon area. Population and economic centers have grown and developed in central Luzon.

Every other language-ethnic group ranks its own group highest, with Tagalog always second. Therefore, through the sum total of the ranking systems, Tagalog is on top as far as the internal ranking is concerned.

Communities are ranked from first class cities to eighth rank towns or communities. Each community knows its rank within the status organization, the rank it is striving for, and what it must do to get there.

Organizations and groups are ranked in the same way. Among service clubs, Rotary, Lions and Jaycees are highest and ranked in that order. Among educational institutions, urban universities are ranked highest, then rural universities, private schools on any level of education and, finally, public schools. The Catholic church is ranked highest of the religious groups, the Muslims next, the Protestant next, and then Iglesia ni Cristo last, though there is potential for the latter to overtake the Protestant groups if the Protestants continue to ignore the upper status people. The Iglesia ni Cristo church is rapidly growing in favor among the masses.[5]

The North American is overwhelmed by the intricate ranking system operating in the Philippines. Even bus lines are ranked, as well as other modes of transportation. This overt ranking is incomprehensible to the American. Taking a plane rather than a train may display a certain amount of ranking but to the American it does not indicate a situation involving bias. Furthermore, the American, as a part of a class system, sees himself with the potential for association on an equal basis with any person or organization which he chooses to relate to for some purpose.

Notes and references

[1] Power and politics in the Philippines are discussed in the following:

John Carroll. *Changing Patterns of Social Structure in the Philippines, 1896–1963*. Ateneo de Manila University Press, Quezon City, 1968, 54–60, 167–180.

Theodore Friend. "Division and Coherence in Philippine Politics," in *Between Two Empires*. Yale University Press, New Haven, 1965.

Jean Grossholtz. *Politics in the Philippines*. Little, Brown and Company, Boston, 1964.

Mary R. Hollnsteiner. *The Dynamics of Power in a Philippine Municipality*. Community Development Research Council, University of the Philippines, Quezon City, 1963.

————. "The Lowland Philippine Alliance System in Municipal Politics." *Philippine Sociological Review*. Vol. 11, No. 3, July, 1962, 167–171.

————. *Manila Microcosm: Leadership, Belonging, and Viewpoints in a Tondo Neighborhood*. Institute of Philippine Culture, Ateneo de Manila University Press, Quezon City, forthcoming IPC publication.

Carl H. Lande. *Leaders, Factions, and Parties: The Structure of Philippine Politics*. Southeast Asia Studies, Monograph Series No. 6, Yale University, 1964.

Willis E. Sibley. "Leadership in a Philippine Barrio." *Philippine Journal of Public Administration*. Vol. 1, No. 2, April, 1957, 154–159.

[2] For further study on the geography and resources of the Philippines, see the following sources:

John Carroll. *Changing Patterns of Social Structure in the Philippines, 1896–1963*. 3–6, 69–76, 1968.

Alden Cutshall. *The Philippines: Nation of Islands*. D. Van Nostrand Company, New York, 1964.

Fred Eggan, et al., Supervisors. *Area Handbook on the Philippines*. University of Chicago for Human Relations Area Files, 1956, 4 volumes.

Joseph E. Spencer. "The Philippines: An Island Borderland," in *Asia East by South*. John Wiley and Sons, New York, 1954, 284–299.

Fredrick L. Wernstedt and J. E. Spencer. *The Philippine Island World: A Physical, Cultural, and Regional Geography*. University of California Press, Berkeley, 1967.

[3] For further study in the area of languages, see also:

Hirofumi Ando. "A Study of the Linguistic Factor in the Philippine Elections." Center for South and Southeast Asian Studies Democratic Development Seminar Working Paper No. 8, December 1966.

Amparo S. Buenaventura. "Some Problems Related to Filipino Multilingualism." *Philippine Sociological Review*. Vol. 11, No. 1–2, January-April, 1963, 142–147.

Ernesto Constantino. *Ilokano Dictionary*. PALI Language Texts Series, Howard McKaughan, editor. University of Hawaii Press, 1971.

Douglas Cretien. "A Classification of Twenty-one Philippine Languages." *The Philippine Journal of Science*. Vol. 91, No. 4, December, 1962.

Fredrick B. Davis. *Philippine Language Teaching Experiments*. Philippine Center for Language Study Monographs, No. 5, Oceana, 1968.

Robert B. Fox. "Language," in *Area Handbook on the Philippines*. University of Chicago for Human Relations Area Files, 1956, 321–355.

F. Landa Jocano. "Language and Socialization: Some Comments on the Process of Cultural Learning." *Culture and Personality*. Filipino Cultural Heritage Lecture Series, No. 3, Gem Publications, Philippine Women's University, Manila, 1966.

Donald N. Larson. "The Philippine Language Scene." *Philippine Sociological Review*. Vol. 11, No. 1–2, January-April, 1963, 4–12.

Teodoro A. Llamzon. *The IPC Guide to Tagalog, Ilocano, Ibanag*. Ateneo de Manila University Press, Quezon City.

———. "The Subgrouping of Philippine Languages." *Philippine Sociological Review*. Vol. 14, No. 3, July, 1966, 145–150.

G. Henry Waterman. "Problems of Syntax in the Translation of the Scriptures in Philippine Dialects." *The Bible Translator*. London, Vol. 11, No. 4, October, 1960, 162–172.

[4] Spanish is still spoken by older people, especially in Zamboanga City, Cauite and sections of Manila. It is also used by politicians. To date, high schools and colleges require that students take it. A prerequisite for an A.B. degree is twenty-four semester hours of Spanish.

[5] For further description of the Iglesia ni Cristo, see:

Hirofumi Ando. "The Iglesia ni Cristo in the 1965 Philippines." Center for South and Southeast Asian Studies Democratic Development Seminar Working Paper No. 3, August 26, 1966.

———. "Study of Iglesia ni Cristo: A Politico-Religious Sect in the Philippines." *Pacific Affairs*. Vol. 42, Fall, 1969, 334–345.

Fred Eggan, et al., Supervisors. *Area Handbook on the Philippines*. 718–728, 1956.

Albert J. Sanders. *A Protestant View of the Iglesia ni Cristo*. Philippine Federation of Christian Churches, Quezon City, 1962.

Julita Reyes Sta. Romana. "Membership and the Norm of Discipline in the Iglesia ni Cristo." *Philippine Sociological Review*. Vol. 3, No. 1, January, 1955, 4–14.

Chapter 6

Status

An interpenetrating social class and status system operates in Filipino society. There are three social classes recognized by the outsider and adhered to by the Filipino. These classes are determined primarily on the basis of behavioral expectations.[1] Examples of the class system—which is distinguished from the status system, the dominant means of grouping or separating people within the society—are given below (see figure 6).

The class system

Upper class behavior is characterized by exceptional, visible wealth—whether or not there is actual basis for such display. A family that has inadvertently lost its wealth will keep up the display as long as possible, using the reciprocating loyalties of the alliance until the "goodwill" runs out and the family is no longer able to reciprocate. This class also makes use of helpers such as a driver and two or more house girls. They use English, wear imported clothes, employ a brusqueness which characterizes interaction (though this does not imply lack of concern), have a potential for travel (especially to the United States), own a vehicle for personal transportation, and have a more formal garden plan or patio than that which characterizes the other two classes. Upper-class people include plantation owners, managers and owners of corporations, highly paid doctors, judges, etc.

Characteristics of middle class behavior include a regular monthly income of four hundred pesos[2] or more as of 1970 (about fifty dollars U. S.), one or two helpers in the house (who do the marketing), certain characteristics of clothing (including a better quality than most though not necessarily imported), women's use of shoes in public rather than slippers, a neat garden but not as formal as those of the upper class (for

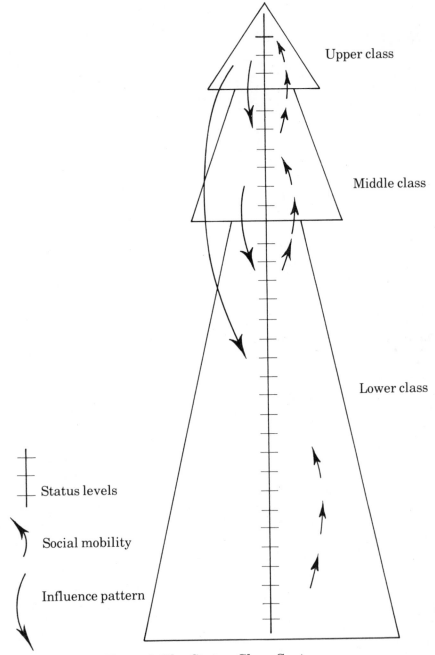

Figure 6. **The Status-Class System**

which the woman is responsible in both classes), and a characteristic house decoration involving pictures. The lower class uses calendar and magazine pictures. Chess playing is generally a middle class activity; land ownership usually involves twenty hectares on the average (49.40 acres); and occupations include lawyers, dentists, professors, small businessmen, pilots, government employees, inspectors and supervisors, higher rank military, and some teachers and pastors.

Members of the lower class earn from two hundred and fifty to four hundred pesos a month, are generally involved in crafts and services, will tend to discuss issues of the day on street corners (rather than in coffee parlors, the home, or office), and play *dama* (a game with twelve stones). Their occupations include driving a jeepney, a tricycle, or a bus; or working as laborers, carpenters, gardeners, or masons. They also might be low-ranked military personnel, pastors, or farmers.[3]

Class designations are generally referred to within conversation. When respondents are pressed to indicate on what class level a person falls, they will give the information, but with reluctance.

The class system is very similar to what the North American has experienced in his own society. Even though he perceives it in subtly different ways than the Filipino, still it is familiar. And, as long as he lives in keeping with class distinctions, he is comfortable with the Filipino and not too obnoxious to him. However, the average North American, taking up residence in the Philippines, sees this behavior distinction as being irrelevant to him. All, or most, of his behavior is in keeping with the middle class practices. Class distinction is delineated in his mind as: upper class—those who do not work, middle class—what "we" are, lower class—the laborer. It also irritates him to be forced to cope with practices and responsibilities which are not in his home setting. For example, any North American may have a house girl or two in keeping with his perceived standing within the Philippine upper class or upper middle class. Few middle class Americans taking up residence in the Philippines rarely, if ever, previously had a maid or a servant even for a short period of time.

The relative ease with which the typical North American accepts the class system, at the same time resisting those expectations which do not characterize American middle class behavior, leaves him vulnerable and basically unable to cope with the entire system. He tends to make the class system the whole and overlook the intricacies of the more important status system that is the final arbiter between people, and through which the specific expectations of behavior are communicated.

The status system

Underlying the class system and providing the foundation for relationships upon which the class system is superimposed is a status system.[4] Every person within Filipino society is at a specific level within the status system. For example, it is as though every person is on a distinct rung of a ladder—the status ladder—in relation to everyone else. Others are either above him or below him in status or community standing. Everyone in the society knows who are above him and who are below him in status. A stranger entering the society or a community is carefully observed for a couple of years to determine his specific strata rank within the community and his relation to individuals. He has up to three years to establish his status. He may do things during this time that will be held against him later. This period of tolerance, however, is designed to let the person learn. If he makes mistakes because of his different background, he must learn by those mistakes and not make them again. An institution may have a slightly longer period of tolerance but it is seen as the composite of the total membership and will be evaluated accordingly. Those encountering the individual or institution will decide on a status ranking in terms of the consistency with which each member follows the expected behavior patterns for a class or status.

Even though every member of the society is on a distinct rung of the status ladder, there is another sense in which every member of the society assumes the status of the head of his particular alliance. This suggests then that every alliance is on a distinct rung of the status ladder in relation to every other alliance. All association between alliances is therefore carried on in light of the respective status levels of the associating alliances. The level of the alliance's status is shared by all associating members and thus reinforces their own personal level. They may even be perceived to be on a higher level than they actually are.

Within the status system, a person wants to associate only with those who are on the same level or higher than himself. This has the potential result of reinforcing his own status level and establishes him on that new level. However, high status people do not want to associate with lower status people for this would undermine their own status base and cause them to be perceived as lower status than they are. Since it is the perception of one's status level that ultimately confirms level, the Filipino pays a great deal of attention to this perception and its cultivation. Anyone seeking a higher status by association up the status ladder becomes a threat to those above him. One who moves into the "wrong" neighborhood, for example, causes everyone within that community to reevaluate his own standing in the community. This process can leave the community disrupted for one to three years until everyone is assured that the perception of his status level is that which he, or his alliance, seeks. Those in an alliance are helped by the rise of a member in status; however, people on the same, or close, level who are not in the alliance may be resentful.

Because of the restrictions imposed upon social interaction by such a system of ranking, the only ones a person or alliance can really associate with are those of lower status rank. The outsome of this relationship is that even though a person might wish to influence someone above him in status, he is basically able to influence only those below himself.

The means of influencing someone of higher status is through associating with someone of higher status than the one to be influenced, someone tied into his alliance through the pattern of reciprocity. This is accomplished through the sponsor or coparent relationship discussed in chapter two. With the birth or marriage of each child, at least one sponsor of higher status than that of the person's alliance is selected. This is not only an honor but also a key to power and influence. Very few Filipinos ever refuse participation in such a relationship.

Social mobility

A large percentage of the people living in a society with a status system attempt to move up in status with every opportunity that comes to them. Many make opportunities to move up and may even accomplish a significant change by such a move. There are five primary means of moving up the status ladder:

(1) By an increase in salary.

(2) By education. Completing high school gives a student potential for a higher status level than that of his family.[5] Provincial college outside of Manila, college or university in Manila, and overseas education move a person further up the ladder. Education gives the person the potential for a higher salary. If he gains this higher salary, he can live on the level of his new status. If he fails to gain it, he is reduced to living on the status level of his family.

(3) By having several higher status sponsors.

(4) Through marriage—particularly useful for girls. Whenever a boy of lower status marries a girl of higher status, a prearranged sum of money changes hands in order to more nearly balance the status level.

(5) By receiving a windfall or winning a lottery and investing part of it. This procedure gives the person the potential for a higher status, but is in reality very difficult to accomplish because of the reciprocal obligation pattern.

Each of these means of upward mobility expresses itself in the political arena. The Philippines, as any Spanish background society, has been so engrossed with politics that politics have become a way of life. Seeking a political position, or other high government office, has been the preoccupation of many Filipinos. The process of gaining political prominence begins at youth as contacts are made and patterns of reciprocity are formed. Positions such as barrio captain, barrio lieutenant, councilor, vice-mayor, mayor, board member, governor, congressman, senator, vice-president, and president give ever successive rise in status. In fact, if one could brag that he has a relative or very close friend of an official (i.e., if he has the "right connection") his status would be raised closer to that of the official. Any kind of connection to an influential person helps one's extended family. Even being personal bodyguard to an official raises one's status.

A person can also move down the ladder through:

(1) Bad judgment—such as continued losses in gambling.

(2) Bad luck—such as an accident which wipes out the finances of the family.

(3) A combination of the two—such as a farmer continuing to over-plant during a drought period.

Security within the status system is achieved by having an extensive association through the alliance and with one's peer group; by having extensive contact with higher statuses through the ritual extension of the family; and by having an extensive network of mutual obligation within statuses lower than one's own. In this way, an accident or a "one time" bad judgment is neutralized. Continued difficulties or errors of judgment ultimately result in the breakup of the alliance when the desire or means of reciprocating are no longer available.[6]

The North American reaction

The average North American sees any status system as status seeking which, to him, is always focused on selfish ends. Indeed, it very frequently is in the United States. There are, however, pockets of status operating in the United States that are not expressions of selfishness but which the North American is so accustomed to that he rarely, if ever, associates them with status. For example, a status relationship exists between the professor and student in the university. If it did not, the student would be unable to learn much from the professor. Both student and teacher can be of the same socioeconomic class but the professor has a higher status toward which the student works and which he ultimately achieves. Once attained, he will relate to his students in keeping with the expectations of the higher status and will seek to maintain this in spite of his former attitude. If the relationship between professor and student breaks down, as it partly did in the sixties when the student tended to ignore or mock his professor, minimum learning results.

Notes and references

[1] For further study, see:

Chester Hunt, et al. "Social Class Structure," *Sociology in the Philippine Setting*. Phoenix Publishing House, Quezon City, 1963. Hunt describes the national system of social classes in terms of both the distribution of wealth in the society and behavior patterns associated with a socioeconomic position.

Frank Lynch. *Social Class in a Bikol Town*. University of Chicago, Chicago, 1959.

[2] Some Filipinos suggest that the limit is 250 pesos, a figure that makes the middle class open to more Filipinos, and may simply be an indication of upward mobility that characterizes the entire society.

[3] Compare also: Edward A. Tiryakian. "The Prestige Evaluation of Occupations in an Underdeveloped Country: The Philippines." *American Journal of Sociology*. Vol. 63, No. 4, January 1958, 390–399.

[4] Insight into the class system of North America and the status system of the Philippines may be obtained by playing *Overpower* and *Strata*. These two behavioral science simulation games are available through The Associates of Urbanus. See the Gaming section of the Bibliography for complete details.

[5] To gain a diploma raises one to a higher status level. Courses like law, medicine, engineering, and other similar ones that give a title after passing the bar or board examination are pursued by thousands of students.

[6] For additional studies relating to social stratification and mobility, see:

Frank Lynch. "Trends Report of Studies in Social Stratification and Social Mobility in the Philippines." *East Asian Cultural Studies*. Vol. 4, No. 1–4, March, 1965, 163–191.

Chapter 7

The Behavior of Status

Manifestations of stratification ranking

In the Philippines the behavior of status is obvious, for it affects everything from the vehicles one travels in to the people with whom one meets and interacts. All areas of the country are status-ranked in relation to Manila, the largest city and highest prestige center. First class cities in every part of the country fall below Manila in prestige but are above all other communities. All communities with any formal organization are ranked below the first class cities—from rank two to rank eight. Every subdivision within a community is ranked. Higher status people live in higher ranked subdivisions and lower status people live in lower ranked areas. These rankings are not necessarily posted. Rather, they are known and will be revealed in conversation.

Higher status people speak English. This is not only due to the recognition the Philippines gave the United States following World War II, but also because the American is high in the stratification hierarchy. People learn English to move up in the system. They speak it to establish their status level, but then revert to their mother tongue. They also speak it to get a higher paying job and thus become eligible for higher status considerations.

Shoes, dress, and shirts are graded by rank. The highest-strata people wear the *barong Tagalog*, a special shirt that compares with the tuxedo of North Americans. A lower strata shirt is the *polo barong*, a sport version of the *barong Tagalog* or *barong Pilipino*[1] and an equivalent of the western type sport jacket. Although the respective shirts are differentiated by price, means of manufacture and location of sale, they are primarily differentiated by dress etiquette. This is known throughout the Philippines and followed carefully.

In marriage arrangements, the lower status family must reimburse the higher status family. This reimbursement covers the potential loss of status risked by the high status family, while the status of the lower family is certain to improve. Usually this is made in some form of financial adjustment, but it may also take the form of property, a dwelling, or a gift.

Hospitality is also extended in keeping with the status system.[2] Those of higher status visiting in a home are served coke, for example, whereas people of lower status are served coffee. Even if there is no coke in the home when higher status people arrive, it is there when the time comes to serve them.

When Filipinos are with elderly people, they are very respectful. They never talk back or openly disagree with their opinions or decisions. Teasing and joking with elders is considered disrespectful and never done. Their permission is asked before leaving the house or before making a decision. It is expected that the decision they have helped to make will be obeyed.

Whenever two Filipinos meet for the first time, a great deal of their early conversation is occupied with information establishing their respective status level in relation to each other. It is not until this is done that some decision is made by both as to just how intense their relationship is to become. Even in introducing people, attention is paid to status, for only the higher status people will be introduced and the lower status people are ignored.

People of higher status are relatively easy to pick out in a group for they have minimum eye contact with ordinary people. The ordinary people stare at them but they do not look back. Generally, higher status people do not initiate friendship, but if they do, ordinary people consider it a big privilege and are proud.

Protecting one's status

Anything that lowers or questions the status of a Filipino hurts him. It might be only a careless gesture from a friend, or a sentence addressed to him that would ordinarily only be addressed to maids or servants—for example, "That's not the way to put the dishes." The Filipino would feel that he was being treated as ignorant and that his status was being threatened. A Tagalog saying is, "Be careful with what you say; you don't know who you are talking with."

The practice of leveling is the means whereby one protects his own status level and reinforces the other's perception of that level. This is done in two ways: (1) Lower status people interacting with higher status people level up. For example, a good friend may say, "You have a lovely new dress." The one complimented would reply, "Oh, it's not new" (whether it is new or not). (2) Higher status people interacting with lower status people level down. For example, a student at the University of Philippines may say to someone in a school of a lower status, "There are rotten eggs in U.P." The non-U.P. student would reply, "Yes, but it is a good school."

People use various means to level including the school they attended, the place or location of that school, the degree they received, their family, and their connections. The North American sees this as a silly practice, for he insists, "If it is a new dress, say so." His is an honesty that implies bluntness and directness. "None of this beating around the bush. They are people, aren't they?" The Filipino has an honesty that permits people of two distinct statuses to be able to converse in a meaningful way within the system. The leveling process in effect calls off the rules of status for that period of encounter.

A person can also practice humility to protect his status. A person of higher status behavior can practice lower class behavior for a short period of time and gain respect. If he continued this practice, however, he would lose respect. This practice protects the non-Filipino stranger within the society who needs to learn the behavior of his status. Medical doctors gain great respect by serving lower status people in their community or in their homes. Were the doctor always to practice with lower status people, however, he would ultimately lose the respect of the higher status people as well as those of lower status.

The authority figure

The primary behavior of status focuses on the authority figure. He may be one's teacher, employer, elder, parent, or some politician. Response to such a figure is always in keeping with the best of taste, the ultimate in decorum and in respect. The person with the highest rank in a group is the authority figure and receives deference.

Whenever the authority figure gets angry, no subordinate can talk back, even to explain his side, unless asked to after the anger or scolding is over. To explain or answer back is to infuriate the authority figure. It only adds fuel to the fire making a bad situation worse. In families, the older brother or sister is the authority figure for the younger ones. The younger ones, knowing that they are subordinates, never attempt to answer back. On the other hand, the authority figure initiates the return of the relationship to normalcy. The boss could do this by giving his subordinates a treat; the teacher by telling a joke to his students; or the older brother or sister by helping the younger ones with their school assignments. The Filipinos consider those who are vocal in their protest to their parents, teachers, elders, or superiors as disrespectful, ill-mannered and ill-bred.

The *teacher* is the authority in the classroom. Everything that he says is the truth and must be accepted. To contradict him would be challenging his authority; to publicly reinforce him by giving added comment would rob him of the respect he deserves. A typical classroom is characterized by all the students silently taking notes as the teacher slowly dictates.

The *politician* is given special treatment by way of meals, accommodations, gifts, favors, and preference. Except for his political opponent and his immediate alliance, everyone views his opinion as the sacred truth. His requests must be heeded. This is why a politician is the finest of intermediaries and a prime target for a sponsor.

The *pastor* cannot behave as a human. He must be extra human since he is expected to be above reproach. Thus, whatever he says in or out of the pulpit is heeded. His biggest mistake may be to be seen angry or doing domestic chores.

The *father* is the head of the household. Children are never to joke with, or tease him because these practices are equated with disrespect. To contradict a father is to insult him. To joke with him is to degrade him by bringing him down to your level. The father puts social distance between himself and his children. The only way they may approach him for anything is through the mother. She is the go-between.

Older siblings are the parental replacement for the younger siblings. When a father dies, or is physically unable to make decisions in the family, the oldest brother or sister (depending upon their education in relation to their mother's) is the authority. In fact, while the parents are out of the house, they leave their "authority" with the older child. He has the right to punish the younger ones and will do so in the following ways: pinch the stomach or the inside part of the thigh, pull the hair near the ears, give a belt on the legs, slap the person (but not on the face), and whip his bottom with leather slippers, firewood, or twigs.

The lawyer and his role

A lawyer in the Philippines behaves differently according to the status of the person, or persons he deals with. He treats those above him in status with great respect and esteem, even to the extent of catering to all their needs if he can. He showers them with favors and gifts. With those of the same status level as himself, there is a reciprocal or symbiotic relationship in which they relate to each other as equals. Those under him in status wait upon him in the same way that he waits upon those of higher status than himself. He receives a wide range of gifts, and favors are extended more in terms of services. He is treated by them with much respect, similarly to the way a magistrate is treated.

A distinction must be made between a lawyer who handles court cases and one who gets an office job where court appearances are not necessary. Such jobs as these are open to him in government or in private business and industry simply because he is a lawyer. Once in a given job, he may not do much that would be classed as legal work.

Being a lawyer is prestigious but being a trial lawyer is even more so. As a trial lawyer, one plays the role of a defender of rights, life, and property. He is the mediator between the party and the courts. He stands before the court as if he were the party himself, against the other lawyer who is expected to act likewise. Because of this, a heated battle is expected inside the courtroom, and at times the lawyers even trade blows. Outside the courtroom, the lawyers could be the best of friends. It is only when there is a confrontation, where the parties represented by the lawyers are present, that the lawyers exhibit a hostile attitude toward each other so the client will feel that he is being earnestly defended. These displays maintain and build status for the trial lawyer who exhibits that behavior. It gives him a high standing with the people and an advantage over a nontrial lawyer.

The lawyer is also an intermediary between the opposing party and his own client. He must deal, however, with the lawyer of the other party and not directly with the other party. In this manner, out-of-court agreements are reached. Amicable settlements are encouraged by the courts, as this frees the courts of unnecessary cases.

In the eyes of the community, a lawyer is seen as a clever tactician and capable of concocting lies. The saying goes, "A lawyer is a liar, and he still lies even when he is dead." A criminal lawyer is more highly regarded if he has not lost any cases, or if he has won most cases. If a lawyer is known to handle large civil cases, he may rank very high. In the cities, corporation lawyers, those versed in taxation or those who have had advanced study abroad command the respect of the community as well as of their own peers.

A lawyer, in general, is *politico* in the sense that he has to conduct his relationship with the public as a politician would. He does his best to maintain a good image in the community, for his public relations should be the very finest. He is extra friendly, attends almost all public and social affairs, circulates, and makes as many acquaintances as possible. Like the politician, he may ascend or descend the social status ladder with ease. He can readily participate in a spontaneous drinking spree with lower status people and they will feel honored. He may even insist on paying the bill if the spree is in a public eating place. He is a talker and stands out in the crowd, a leader and everyone looks to him for guidance and counsel. He is one who cannot only maintain his status, but can reinforce it by accepting money, produce, or land as legitimate remuneration. He gets along with everyone and is looked up to by the community. It is no wonder that most elective positions are filled by lawyers.

Gift giving and the lawyer

When a lawyer gives a gift to one above him in status, he has to be very selective with his choice. The quality of the gift must be appropriate to the status rank of the person receiving the gift. For example, the president of the country must receive the highest quality gift. Similarly, expensive gifts are given to senators, congressmen, governors, and mayors. Also, the occasion to give the gift must be carefully chosen—such as birthdays, weddings, anniversaries, Christmas, the wedding of a child, etc. Gifts vary from expensive wrist watches (Rolex or Omega), cuff links, fountain pens, and attaché cases to *barong Tagalog* (cloth), and other similar gifts. One lawyer who was the speaker of the house was even known to receive automobiles.

Gift receiving and the lawyer

Besides the gifts the lawyer gives the higher status person, he also receives gifts. The more prominent a lawyer is in the community, the more gifts he will receive from his immediate family, close relatives, friends, and clients (especially Chinese, individuals in business, private companies, partnerships, or business establishments). The occasion is chosen carefully. Types of gifts include expensive clothes such as a fur coat for the very highest status[3] or food stuffs such as ham, cheese balls, grapes, apples, wine, or liquor. The gifts are given in keeping with the lawyer's status ranking within the community. The higher his status, the more expensive the gifts.

The gift giver sacrifices a great deal to give a gift. Besides the cost of the gift, it is sent by messenger unless the occasion is a party given to celebrate a birthday, anniversary, or wedding. In that case the gift is carried by the giver to the celebration.

Notes and references

[1] The difference between who wears the *barong Pilipino* and *polo barong*, though once a definitive factor in status behavior, is not always a satisfactory indicator today. Rather status distinction today is signaled by how the shirt is worn, what material or kind of cloth it is made of, and where it was purchased. If the shirt were bought in Quiapo

(Manila) it would be known as low class; but if in Escolta (also Manila) then it would be perceived to be of high quality.

[2] The Filipino's term "floor leader" means that the host couple is likely to sleep on the floor, giving up their bed for a higher status visitor. The "second floor leader" is another couple on the floor as well because they are still lower than the other visitor but not necessarily lower than the host couple.

[3] The Elizaldes, Ayalas, and their kin are an example of those who reside in Forbes Park.

Chapter 8

Reciprocity

Reciprocity illustrated

A man received a loan from the Social Security system for twelve thousand pesos to improve his farm. The loan was meant for farm improvement. His close friend and *compadre* approached him and asked to borrow eight thousand pesos of it for a very urgent need, and the man loaned this large sum to him. A North American friend of the two men could not understand the reason for this transaction and felt sorry for the lender. As far as the lender was concerned, there was no problem. He was glad he could aid his friend since their relationship was far more important to him than his farm. The improvement could wait.

Varying reciprocity exchanges

The alliance system provides a network of supporters to the individual (ego), and is crucial to his gaining and maintaining power. These supporters provide a network of reciprocal relationships. Members of an alliance extend and expect mutual assistance and loyalty.[1]

... a kinsman, a *compadre*, a neighbor, or a friend is emotionally close, ... an ally, that can really be counted on. His well-being becomes the well-being of the group, and the group's collective welfare becomes his welfare. Allies can shift ... since one who does not prove his loyalty in time of need is cast aside, ... new close relationships are constantly being formed as circumstances activate potential alliance ties.[2]

Reciprocal relationships become the operating principle within Philippine society. They activate the relationship wherein every favor, gift, or service extended to another is repaid according to the statuses of the people involved and the nature of the exchange.

There are three forms of reciprocity exchanges: (1) contractual reciprocity; (2) quasi-contractual reciprocity; and (3) *utang na loob* (debt of
gratitude) reciprocity.

• *Contractual reciprocity* is an arrangement between two or more
people to do a task for a specific remuneration at some specified time.
This remuneration can be financial or mutual assistance. The agreements
are already established beforehand. This could be illustrated by a group
of farmers who help each other plow their fields. An approximately equal
amount of work is done on each farm, and when the rotation is complete
all obligations have been met.

The nature of this system is one of mutual assistance with each
participant knowing exactly what is expected of him, as well as knowing
what he may expect of the others.

Hollnsteiner summarizes contractual reciprocity as,

> ... the reciprocal acts are equivalent, their amount and form having been
> explicitly agreed upon beforehand. ... Fulfillment of the contract is such that
> there is no doubt in the mind of either party that payment has been made;
> repayment is unmistakable. The reciprocation terminates that particular
> relationship, leaving the participants in a state of equilibrium.[3]

• *Quasi-contractual reciprocity* regulates balanced exchange where the
terms of repayment are not explicitly stated, but are equal in value. For
example, if a person is asked to help move a house, he can ask the other
person to reciprocate by helping him move his house.

• *Utang na loob* encompasses an important system of reciprocal obligation and behavioral expectations. This system regulates and operates the
limits of socially meaningful relations among individuals, determines the
nature of relationships, and holds the key to understanding bilateral
social organization, structure, and process. Through *utang na loob* a favor
will initiate a relationship but there is no set or established return for
that favor. In some way, the debt of gratitude must be returned with
interest.

Principles of reciprocal obligation

Charles Kaut in his article on *utang na loob* gives the most accurate
model of this system.[4] He discusses the four basic principles necessary to
understand the system of reciprocal obligation. These are: (1) the concept
of the gift and volition, (2) the concept of acceptance, (3) the necessity of
repaying the gift, and (4) the manner of evaluating the need and surplus.

• The first principle for reciprocal obligation is that a theoretically
voluntary and disinterested gift establishes a unilateral obligation or
state of indebtedness between giver and receiver.

Filipinos give gifts on special occasions: a short while after a request has been granted, when asking a favor, in strengthening friendships, and in pacifying an angry person. Occasions calling for gifts are Christmas, birthdays, graduations, *pasalobong* (a gift brought from a trip), when passing a bar or board exam, an expression of thoughtfulness, appreciation or friendship. These are good occasions to remember godchildren and godparents, and are good times to show gratitude for a favor or request granted if the timing is in keeping with the principle of favor reciprocity.

It is proper to wait a little after a request has been granted or a favor given before giving a gift. If someone were to get a job through the aid of an intermediary, he would wait until he received his first salary before buying a gift for his benefactor. If someone could afford to give a gift as soon as the job was arranged for, before the first salary, it would still be proper to wait three to five days before extending a gift. It is important, however, for the person receiving the job to go immediately to the intermediary and verbally express his appreciation. This is done his first day in the office. Gifts are lubricants which aid the granting of the requested favor.

Friendships can be strengthened any time. One way is to bring a *pasalobong* after a trip. Or, if a person had a party and a friend was unable to attend, the hostess would carry cakes, roast pig, or other food to their home the next morning.

Gifts are not perceived by the Filipino as goods wrapped up in nice paper and tied with ribbons; rather, they are anything that is given to another person. On occasion they need to be wrapped, but formal wrapping does not accompany all gifts. For example, one person related the following incident:

> I stayed overnight in the homes of two of my friends. One gave me two Avon perfumes and the other gave me a towel set. The mother of the friend who gave me a towel set was not satisfied with that as a gift, and so gave me some money before I left.

Gifts are also used to pacify an angry person but they are channeled through an intermediary who can reinforce the apology. Lovers will use gifts to restore their relationship following a quarrel.

• The second principle is that the acceptance of a commodity or service from another person constitutes a virtual contract. Because of the threat of rejection, an individual will make every effort to ascertain the probability of acceptance before offering a gift. Rejection means shame (*hiya*) and vengeance. Consequently, the giver will try to make sure that the person to whom he wishes to give a present is within his obligation system. He will also check to see if the recipient is capable of repaying the gift.

• The third principle of repayment or reciprocation of the gift, can be divided into two distinct categories: repayments made upon demand which can never in themselves end the debt situation; and unsolicited reciprocation which is freewill in nature, and is itself a gift which will reverse or modify the direction of the debt.

Generally, one does not refuse offers of help, gifts (except for wine and cigarettes), or honor (being asked to be godparents). Friends and close relatives do not refuse each other unless there has been a strain in the relationship causing them to become cold and impersonal, in which case there is a polite refusal. For example, Mothers A and B had a strained relationship, but their daughters were good friends. A's daughter invited B's daughter and her friends to her house for dinner. But Mother B instructed her daughter to refuse the invitation, which she did. However, in normal cases among friends, a very sincere (though usually lengthy) explanation is needed to explain the refusal.

• The fourth principle involves need and surplus. The creditor must have a recognized need for whatever is being requested and the debtor must be in a position of having a recognized surplus.

An important factor in this principle is that when someone has an obvious need, he will not be helped by members of his social grouping unless he solicits that aid. There are three reasons why this would lead to shame. To volunteer aid would cause embarrassment by calling attention to his need, by not allowing him to solve his problems on his own initiative, and by putting him in the position of further indebtedness to the benefactor.

Reciprocal relationships

Need and surplus are expressed in reciprocal relationships involving sharing, borrowing-loaning and mutual assistance.

Food is shared in the Filipino setting. This sharing is done within the family, at meals when someone else is present, within the community when there is a need, or after a party when there are leftovers. Clothing—such as pants, shirts, undershirts, blouses, skirts, jeans, dresses, and even shoes—is also shared. A brother shares his belongings with another brother, a sister with a sister. Usually families that cannot afford to buy every member of the family something personal for himself end up with a beautiful sharing relationship. However, such a practice can be a source for trouble if, for example, one sister awakens with the intent to wear a specific dress and finds that her sister has the same idea.

Filipinos will invite friends to eat with them when they come just in time for lunch or supper. Visitors will even invite themselves to stay by teasingly suggesting, "It is good timing for lunch, isn't it?" The self-invitation is done very subtly. The other person is expected to respond and say, "That's right, how about eating lunch at home?" Then the host retracts this and later agrees. It does not matter what is on the table, the point is the food and fellowship.

Visits are always linked with eating. Every visitor is offered something to eat—a snack, coffee, coke, or native food. Even if the visitor is in a hurry, he is urged to eat something; if he has just eaten, he will still be offered more. Rejection of food proffered would signify rejection of the home and even of the person offering it.

It is generally considered inhospitable if no food is offered within the first fifteen to thirty minutes. If a host finally offers food after an hour, he is considered unkind and stingy. Hospitality extended is the same no matter what the business or concern of the visit. A Filipino lady said,

> My mother, my sister, and I went to visit a relative and they did not even offer a glass of water. Mother said that the cups in that house are turned down, meaning that the home is not hospitable. Mother has to have a twenty-four hour coffee pot and instant coffee besides to keep up with the people who come to chat, look for jobs, or just visit.

North Americans do not have to offer food to visitors in their homes in order to be hospitable though they often offer coffee. Usually if they do offer food, it is in relation to a planned occasion rather than a drop-in visit. Anyone showing up at mealtime is considered a freeloader and not invited to stay for the meal. The meal is delayed until the visitor leaves. If an invitation is extended to someone in the home at mealtime, only one invitation is given. But the Filipino will not respond affirmatively until after two or three specific invitations are given for he does not want to appear piggish. The American's primary means of extending an invitation to a meal or snack is by a formal invitation, whereas the Filipino likes the on-the-spot approach better.

When a Filipino loans something, it means he can do without it for a considerable length of time. If he needs it, he goes and gets it. The borrower, therefore, feels free to keep that item until the original owner claims it. The borrower may also loan the item to a friend. If the item is not to be loaned further, the original owner specifies the day he will get it. The North American, on the other hand, may loan something but expects the borrower to be responsible for it and return it promptly without the owner chasing it down.

Mutual assistance is carried out when neighboring families build a building, plant a field, or harvest the crops. The expectation is that this service will be reciprocated when the need arises, and will take precedence over all other obligations, even on Sunday. The participants are fed with abundant food and the experience shared becomes more like the rural barn building events of early America.

Notes and references

[1] For additional background material on the concept of reciprocity, see:

Claude Levi-Strauss. "The Principle of Reciprocity." *Sociological Theory: A Book of Readings*. Lewis Coser and Bernard Rosenberg, editors. The MacMillan Company, New York, 1957, 84–94.

Bronislaw Malinowski. "Reciprocity and Obligation," in *Man and Society*. Jerome Manis and Samuel Clark, Editors. Macmillan, New York, 1960.

[2] Mary R. Hollnsteiner. *The Dynamics of Power in a Philippine Municipality*. Community Development Research Council, University of the Philippines, Quezon City, 1963, 63.

[3] ———. 389.

[4] Charles Kaut. "*Utang na Loob*: A System of Contractive Obligation Among Tagalogs." *Southwestern Journal of Anthropology*. Vol. 17, No. 3, 1961, 258–259. (Also contained in *Social Structure and Value Orientation*. Edited by F. Landa Jocano.)

Chapter 9

The Reciprocal Relationship

Developing a relationship

Utang na loob relationships have three possible stages of development (see figure 7).

In the first there is an initial presentation through which an obligation relationship is activated: *Utang na loob* is created.

Following this may come a relatively unstable phase wherein indebtedness alternates back and forth between two individuals through reciprocal giving and repayment.

The third possible stage is a culmination of a long, intimate, and active obligation association; complete reciprocity of mutual support and aid so that two individuals become complementary *utang na loob* partners. In this stage, one is never exclusively in debt to the other but, rather, they are co-equally indebted (*kautang na loob*).[1]

Before one can ask a favor, he must establish a friendly relationship. He can do this either directly or indirectly by using an intermediary who is a good friend of the person from whom he wishes to ask the favor. It could happen as follows.

Fred must leave for Manila immediately but does not have a plane seat and has to go stand-by. He goes to a banker friend, Mr. Tomale, who approves loans. One such loan went to Mr. Fuentes, manager of the Philippine Air Lines Operations in Fred's town. Mr. Fuentes will do anything for Mr. Tomale in gratitude for the recent approval of a loan. The result is that Fred will get the plane seat that he needs.

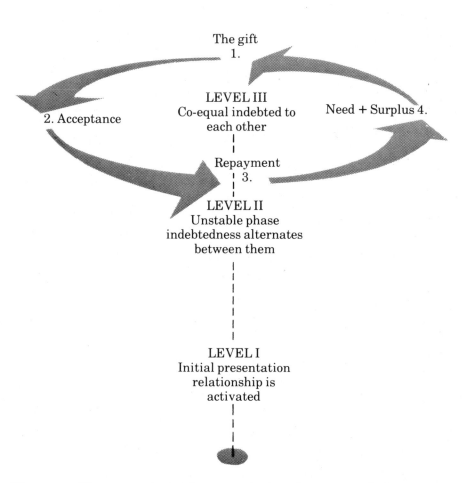

The gift
1.

LEVEL III
Co-equal indebted to
each other

Need + Surplus 4.

2. Acceptance

Repayment
3.

LEVEL II
Unstable phase
indebtedness alternates
between them

LEVEL I
Initial presentation
relationship is
activated

Figure 7. Utang na loob: **Stages of Development of Contractual Obligation**

How to make a request: Type I

In the United States, if John wished to borrow a dollar from Peter he would probably say, "Hey, Pete, lend me a buck, will you? I'll pay you back tomorrow." Pete would respond, "Sure John, here."

In the Philippines, however, that same type of request would be much more complicated. It would involve an opening greeting, an introduction to the request, and finally the request itself. For example:

Juan: Good morning, Pedro.

Pedro: Good morning, Juan.

Juan: How are you? You look happy.

Pedro: I'm very fine. I just received a registered letter from home with my allowance for the month.

Juan: Oh, really! Good for you. I haven't received mine yet and I'm a bit worried since today is the last day to pay our dorm fees.

Pedro: Oh, that's too bad. How much do you have to pay?

Juan: Twenty pesos. That's why I'm really ashamed to borrow from you but I have no choice. If it's not too shameful, I should like to borrow twenty pesos.

Pedro: Oh, sure, here's twenty pesos. Just pay me immediately when your allowance arrives. Okay?

Juan: Thanks a lot. By the way, when are we going swimming again? It's been a long time since we went together.

Pedro: Oh, as soon as we have time, we'll go.

Juan: Well, thanks again. Good-bye.

Pedro: Good-bye.

The greeting is first, then the feeler. When the Filipino is sure of a favorable reception, he is ready to work toward the main request. A secondary request may be introduced at this point as a softening influence, for example, "How about going swimming some day?" or, "How about playing basketball?" This preliminary small talk will be picked up again after the main request is presented, permitting the subject to be changed as soon as possible after the request. It is not proper to dwell on the request. The prerequest small talk may take an hour or more, whereas the postrequest conversation terminates in a couple of minutes. If the request is made where refreshments can be served, it is customary to have them because of the lengthy prerequest period.[2]

How to make a request: Type II

Mrs. Flores wants to borrow twenty pesos for her granddaughter's boat fare to the province. She enters and sits in the living room while

63

Mrs. Bulante does odd jobs in the kitchen. They talk loudly because of the distance between them. Mrs. Flores is enjoying the snacks provided by Mrs. Bulante.

Mrs. Flores: (Knocks on door.) Good morning!

Mrs. Bulante: Oh! Mrs. Flores, it's you. Good morning. Come in!

Mrs. Flores: Thank you.

Mrs. Bulante: Sit down! Sit down!

Mrs. Flores: How are you?

Mrs. Bulante: Fine.

Mrs. Flores: Where are your sister's children?

Mrs. Bulante: They are picnicking because today is a holiday.

Mrs. Flores: Oh, that's right. Where is your husband?

Mrs. Bulante: Upstairs reading. Just keep on talking while I prepare some snacks.

Mrs. Flores: Oh, never mind the *merienda* (coffee break). It's still early.

Mrs. Bulante: No, it's already ten o'clock. What do you like, coke or Truorange?

Mrs. Flores: Truorange will do. Are you not pregnant yet?

Mrs. Bulante: No, not yet. We are hoping I will be soon.

Mrs. Flores: Are you using birth control?

Mrs. Bulante: No, we are not.

Mrs. Flores: Then why haven't you conceived yet? You have been married about a year now. That's too long. Did you have yourself examined to see who is defective?

Mrs. Bulante: No, we will just wait until I am pregnant.

Mrs. Flores: Well, I know of couples who have their first pregnancy after five to eight years. But this birth control is really not good. It causes cancer and usually the husband gallivants. If you don't have children you will be sad since your husband will play around.

Mrs. Bulante: Well, it is my husband who is the defective one then. It isn't my fault. Come on, have some more crackers.

Mrs. Flores: Thank you. Where is your husband working? The same place?

Mrs. Bulante: Yes, he is still in the civil service department.

Mrs. Flores: That's good. If he stays with the government, he will get retirement pay.

Mrs. Bulante: Yes, that's what we figure.

Mrs. Flores: How much is he earning now? Perhaps a thousand or more?

Mrs. Bulante: No, he is not earning that much. Just enough for us.

Mrs. Flores: How about you? Being a teacher in the college you must be receiving big, too. How much is your salary?

Mrs. Bulante: Oh, just enough to pay for this apartment and to help with the tuition of my brother in college. Their tuition is so high now, and just this month our landlord raised the rent by twenty pesos. We are really hard up now.

Mrs. Flores: My! If people having a salary are having a hard time, how much more for me when I don't have regular income. Why don't you come to the house sometime? My fruit trees are full of fruit and my garden is really producing vegetables.

Mrs. Bulante: Yes, I may one of these days.

Mrs. Flores: You know, my granddaughter has been vacationing here with me for a month. You know, the daughter of my youngest daughter, Nelly.

Mrs. Bulante: Yes, how long will she be staying with you?

Mrs. Flores: Well, really—this is the reason why I came over to see you today—she wants to go home tomorrow because she feels lonely now. But I don't have any money for her boat fare. I tried to see my *compadre* (godparent) in the Williams Steamship Navigation office last night to ask for a pass but he said I came too late since all passes have been issued and there won't be any bed space left because it is vacation time and all the people are traveling.

Mrs. Bulante: Oh, that's too bad.

Mrs. Flores: So I decided to let her take another boat. She has been crying all night as she is really lonely now. So even if we have to pay twenty pesos, we will do it. I pity her. She misses her parents so.

Mrs. Bulante: Yes, I understand. But really, you seem not to have good luck because I just paid my brother's tuition yesterday.

Mrs. Flores: Really, if I were not in such dire need, I would not come to you because it is shameful.

Mrs. Bulante: Really now, I don't have any money but if your granddaughter can wait till the end of the month, perhaps I can lend you some after I get my salary. Try to comfort your granddaughter. Let her come here. Perhaps my sister's children can take her with them to their parties.

Mrs. Flores: Okay. I will do that. Really, children nowadays are not like the children of our times. They are attached too much to their parents. When I was young, I was gone from our home for months and months and did not cry for my parents.

Mrs. Bulante: Yes, children nowadays are very dependent on their parents.

Mrs. Flores: Now, I'll have to go because you might have some things to do. I disturbed you. I am sorry.

Mrs. Bulante: Oh, don't worry. It's all right. Just come back at the end of the month.

Mrs. Flores: Okay. Thank you. Good-bye.

Mrs. Bulante: Good-bye.

Initiation of obligation

There are two primary functions of this system of mutual obligation. The first involves the distribution of wealth, while the second builds interpersonal loyalties. There are seven "favors" extended that initiate expected repayment at some time in the future. These are:

(1) Financing the education of an individual, placing him under an obligation to show concern, give money, provide an education for another, extend services (helping in the house), or show kindnesses (responding promptly to some request).

(2) Enabling someone to hold office. This is repaid by gifts of money or clothes, by giving a party for the supporters, or by securing a job for another.

(3) Lending money, property, or personal possessions.

(4) Giving gifts at Christmas time.

(5) Extending manual, professional, or personal services.

(6) Saving someone's life, protecting them from harm, or saving possessions from fire.

(7) Being a sponsor at a baptism or wedding.

Most favors are repayable either to the person extending the favor or to another to whom you can extend the same favor. But the debt to parents, or the saving of one's life, is the kind that can never be fully repaid.

Hollnsteiner gives an overall summary of the three kinds of reciprocity in her chart.[3]

An imbalance in the behavioral system: *hiya*

When the system of reciprocity is out of balance or malfunctioning, a person becomes embarrassed, shamed, or humiliated. *Hiya* is the sanction which reinforces the desirability of feeling and honoring *utang na loob.*

The English translation of the word *hiya* has been "shame." However, its meaning appears to follow a continuum—the scale of response moves in intensity from shyness, timidity, embarrassment, sensitivity to severe forms of shame, and humiliation.[4]

As a result of a workshop of Filipino teachers and Peace Corps volunteers in Iloilo, the following interpretation of *hiya* was made by Jaime C. Bulatao.

Hiya may be defined as a painful emotion arising from a relationship with an authority figure or with society, inhibiting self-assertion in a situation which is perceived as dangerous to one's ego. It is a kind of anxiety, a fear of being left exposed, unprotected, and unaccepted. It is a fear of abandonment, of 'loss of soul,' of one's life, but of something perceived as more valuable than life itself, namely the ego, the self.[5]

What is the condition that develops *hiya* within the personality (ego)? Bulatao attributed this shyness to an unindividuated ego, a self so organically attached to its primary group that it does not easily function as an individual. Such a person feels insecure. He prefers to be a part of a group.

A person embedded in his own social group will seek security in the families; namely, his family when he is a child and the alliance when he is an adult. The family and alliance system are closely knit. They are the center of ego's familiarity. If he must perform a task as an individual, all group support withdrawn, he feels great anxiety. He does not want to stand out as an individual.

Hiya arises in close, highly intradependent, small groups. Strong emphasis on close family ties and fostering dependency within the family is an important part of the *hiya* system. Child-rearing practices and attitudes are credited as being the main factor in forming the Filipino personality. A mother identifies with her child. She exercises tight control and curbs his independence. His sense of being an individual is overpowered by the group relationship.

Personalism is another important trait of the *hiya* system, for it is upon personal relations that the ego places its security. Face-to-face contact is very important.

Sensitivity to another's feelings is also important. It will make a Filipino send an intermediary first to explore the feelings of the person from whom he seeks to obtain a favor. The intermediary reinforces the petition and prevents *hiya* in case the petition is denied.

Sensitivity to the opinions of others, especially those who carry weight in the community, is likewise important. Because of this sensitivity, the individual's actions and values will change outwardly. His values and actions may be the expression of his environment, not necessarily his own personal convictions.

The external norm of conduct makes an "inner" and "outer" situation and sets the stage for the phenomenon known as split-level.[6] The split occurs when the individual is a member of two groups, each requiring conformity to its own behavioral demands. An example of a split-level situation is that of home and school. A student will identify with his home group when at home, with his school group when at school, conforming to the demands of each without finding it inconsistent.

Hiya forces the individual to conform to the expectations of two semiopposed groups when two convictions exist. One conviction is couched in abstract terms of the world outside his alliance, the other is in concrete terms of his family. In order to prevent *hiya*, the Filipino feels that distance from the authority figure is most comfortable.

The problem for the Filipino is to be aware that he has two inconsistent norms and that he must overcome this split if he is to become a mature person (see figure 8).

When looking into the behavior of *hiya*, one begins to understand what happens when the system of reciprocity is out of balance or malfunctioning. A person's embarrassment, shame, or humiliation depends upon the intensity of his involvement. Such shame may be acted upon immediately, or it may continue through an extensive period of time.

The intensity of humiliation is determined by the number of people involved and the degree of involvement with them. The result of humiliation is retribution. The greater the humiliation, the more intense the retribution.

The degree of humiliation is shown in the following intensity scale of response: mild—cut off the friendship; not so mild—'damn' the other people; obvious reprisal—theft or destruction of possessions; extreme response—bodily harm; very extreme response—murder.

A common Filipino expression runs this way: "I would rather that you kill me than to put me to shame." To be shamed in public is terribly humiliating, and revenge is the logical action for the Filipino. For serious offenses, if a murder is not committed then a "counter-shame" is enacted; for example, disgracing a daughter or sister of an offender.

A ship captain was asked, "What if you found out that your wife shamed your family name by having illicit relations with another man?" "Killing her is too mild. I would undress her naked and parade her in the market and put her to shame," he answered.

An explanation of the system

Combining several illustrations cited, the principle *hiya* will be broken down according to bicultural models: vulnerability is a weakness, status and authority, and a conflict model.

• *Vulnerability is a weakness.* Through most of his life, the Filipino is very sensitive to vulnerability—to showing the weakness of erring—and

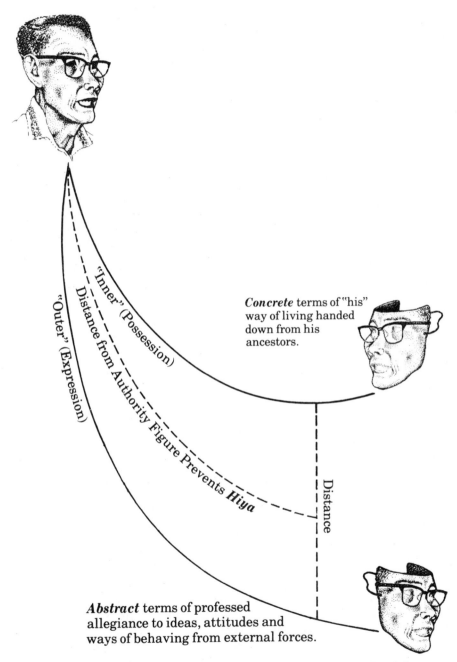

"Inner" (Possession)
Distance from Authority Figure Prevents *Hiya*

"Outer" (Expression)

Concrete terms of "his" way of living handed down from his ancestors.

Distance

Abstract terms of professed allegiance to ideas, attitudes and ways of behaving from external forces.

Figure 8. **Two Convictions Existing One on Top of the Other**

he works within society to cover all such evidence. Note the following examples from Bulatao:

> A ten-year-old girl is asked to sing in front of a group. At the end of the song she is vigorously applauded. She sits down, digs her fingers into her cheeks and her knuckles into her eyes as if wanting to cry. After a minute, when the attention has shifted from her, she returns to normal.
>
> . . . .
>
> A shy young man of twenty is interviewed for an hour in front of the assembled group. . . . At the end of the interview he is asked how he feels. "I do not feel very good," he says. "Why not?" he is asked. "Because now you know that I am different." "What do you mean, different?" "I mean that now you know that I am different from you."[7]

From the two illustrations above, the following observations were drawn by the members attending the Peace Corps workshop.[8]

(1) *Hiya* is a painful emotion and involves a fear or sense of inadequacy in threatening situations.

(2) *Hiya* produces a need to conform with the expectation of an authority figure or with society. There is a need to be hidden in and accepted by the group.

(3) *Hiya* is soul-shaking because the danger is to the ego itself, not to a segment of the personality. The worth of the self is questioned.

• *Status and authority*. Status is perceived in an authority figure. It includes the attitudes, values, and behavior ascribed by the society. When the presence of an authority figure threatens an individual's evaluation of himself, *hiya* occurs. Bulatao notes:

> A college student is talking to his teacher in the teacher's lounge. The bell for class rings unnoticed by the teacher. Though the boy knows that he will be late for class, he does not tell the teacher but waits for him to make the first move. When asked later why he acted the way he did, he answers, "I was ashamed to you."[9]

The following observations were drawn from this illustration:[10]

(1) *Hiya* is only felt in a face-to-face encounter with another person, and it must involve a relationship with another whose opinion is important.

(2) This other person is perceived as an authority figure. His approval is supportive and lends a feeling of worth, but disapproval arouses anxiety about one's self-worth.

(3) The word "shame" is used in different ways by Filipinos and Americans. A Filipino's "I am ashamed of you" is quite different from the American's "I am ashamed of myself." The painful emotion of *hiya* is probably closer to embarrassment than shame.

• *Conflict model.* When a conflict situation arises, the immediate tendency is to escape from the anxiety-creating situation. A child escapes by hiding; an adult by freezing. Jaime Bulatao gives an example of each type of escape.[11] A small child hid his face when asked to greet a guest. An adult on a TV amateur show spoke very low and said little while being questioned by the toastmaster. But during his act he performed with all the gusto that was expected of him.

Another conflict situation arises when one is caught in a socially unacceptable act. *Hiya* results from being caught, not from the act itself.

If a person fails in his obligation to show respect to another and insults him instead, the second could personally attack him if under the influence of liquor. Otherwise, he might remember the insult years later.

In summary, *hiya* is the counter system of thrust-humiliation and it operates from two points of reference: a person fails to meet an obligation, or the other person humiliates the one to whom he has an obligation.

The North American reaction

The North American has his own system of reciprocal obligation. The biggest difference lies in the fact that most services which fall in the category of *utang na loob* (debt of primary obligation) for the Filipino are paid contractual services for the North American. Also, loans of money and personal possessions are more formal in the States. Money loans are arranged with money institutions, e.g. banks, small loan offices, savings and loan services; loans of personal property are arranged with one person who is personally responsible for that item. Both money and possessions must be returned intact and, in the case of money, with sufficient interest to cover the risk entailed.

The North American does have a system of reciprocal obligation operating in a very restricted sphere and involving a minimum of occasions and items. However, he resists entering into any obligation in most instances because he will no longer feel free to come and go. Such an obligation lies heavy on him. Also, any request for a personal loan is reacted to as taking advantage of a friendship.

Notes and references

[1] Charles Kaut. "*Utang na Loob*: A System of Contractual Obligation among Tagalogs." *Southwestern Journal of Anthropology.* Vol. 17, No. 3, 1961, 266.

[2] It is also interesting to note that persuasion experiments in the field of social psychology have shown that people are more persuadable when eating.

[3] Mary R. Hollnsteiner. "Reciprocity in the Lowland Philippines," in *Four Readings in Philippine Values*, 42. (Also in *Philippine Studies Quarterly*, 406.)

[4] For further discussion of *hiya*, see:

A LOOK AT FILIPINO LIFESTYLES

Milton L. Barnett. "*Hiya*, Shame and Guilt: Preliminary Consideration of the Concepts vs. Analytical Tools for Consideration of Philippine Social Science." *Philippine Sociological Review*. Vol. 15, 1966, 276–291.

Jaime Bulatao. "*Hiya*." *Philippine Studies*. Vol. 12, No. 3, July, 1964, 424–438.

————. "The *Hiya* System in Filipino Culture," in *Structure and Value Orientation*. Edited by F. Landa Jocano.

Rachel Hare. "Autonomy, Dependency and Problem Solving in Filipino Children," in *Modernization: Its Impact in the Philippines IV*. IPC Papers, No. 7. Ateneo de Manila University Press, Quezon City, 1969.

F. Landa Jocano. *Growing up in a Philippine Barrio*. 1969, 98–99.

Frank Lynch. "Social Acceptance," in *Four Readings on Philippine Values*. 16–17.

[5] Jaime Bulatao. "The *Hiya* System in Filipino Culture," in *Structure and Value Orientation*. Edited by F. Landa Jocano. Filipino Cultural Heritage Lecture Series, No. 2, General Publications, Philippine Women's University, Manila, 1966, 28.

[6] Jaime Bulatao discusses a manifestation of the "split-level" in relation to Christian ideals in "Split-Level Christianity." *Split-Level Christianity (and) Christian Renewal of Philippine Values*. Ateneo de Manila University Press, Quezon City, 1966.

[7] Bulatao. "*Hiya*." 425–426.

[8] ————. 426.

[9] ————. 425.

[10] ————. 427.

[11] ————. 424–425.

Chapter 10

The Role of the Intermediary

Spontaneous mediation

Loarca, in his book on the relationships existing among the islands, stated that in 1582 the people of Panay had no judges. Instead, they had mediators who went from one party to another to bring about reconciliations. Thus the Spanish concept of intermediary was not only taken at face value; it was incorporated smoothly and naturally into the lives of the Filipinos.

Intermediaries, or mediators, are as old as Filipino society itself. They occupy an influential, prominent role in the life of the Filipino. No one acts in a formal way as mediator except when it concerns labor unions, employee conflict, or disagreement between two nations, two parties or two organizations regarding policies and practice. The North American is familiar with this mediation and understands how it works. However, other mediatory acts are also done naturally and spontaneously in the Philippines which the North American finds difficult to comprehend. But mediation is a vital part of the everyday life of a Filipino. Every Filipino has either mediated or been a party to a conflict where informal mediation was used.

Good, close friends always function as intermediaries during courtship, lovers' quarrels, marital spats, job hunting, asking for favors, or asking for one's hand in marriage.[1] Usually, in such cases the person is not asked to be the intermediary. The good friend will simply take it upon himself to function that way as a gesture of concern and assistance. People in status relationship to another person, on the other hand, will approach him directly, in keeping with the specific nature of the relationship—godparent or sponsor, or higher status but nonassociating family member.

An intermediary is a good friend of both parties. He is supposed to be neutral, although he appears to take sides when he is with either of the parties. The North American sees him as being two-faced, but, in effect, he is simply exhibiting a "broker's behavior" as he represents both parties to a degree, though he is not rewarded with cash for his efforts.

When the intermediary is used

A Filipino employs an intermediary in two basic capacities: preventive or remedial. The preventive service of the intermediary is used to avoid embarrassment such as when a person needs information to act, when an unpleasant message must be communicated to another, when there is need to influence someone of higher status, when one is sure his request will be turned down, or whenever it is apparent that someone will be embarrassed by a comment or request. The remedial service is rendered to pacify existing conflict or to remedy a long-standing disagreement.

• *Making an embarrassing request.* Any time one has to borrow money it is perceived as potentially embarrassing, especially if a large sum has been previously borrowed. The embarrassment is lessened when approaching a friend, but is increased with someone of higher status. The person needing the money feels the *hiya* or shame of facing the other person who can lend him money. To sidestep this shame situation, he looks for someone who is on the same level as the lender. He asks this person to be intermediary and do the asking for him. The intermediary (who, hopefully, has good connections) approaches the person with the money and presents the request. He dare not do this, even yet, in a straightforward manner but gradually leads up to the request. The one lending the money could be a wealthy godfather. In that case, the parents would act as intermediaries for their son or daughter. Or, it could be a wealthy businessman, and a high status godfather would be called upon to make the request.

• *A threatened elopement.* If there is the threat of an elopement, the entire family could be embarrassed so an intermediary is employed. In most cases, the couple will go to their godparents or to an older influential member of the family or alliance, e.g., an uncle or the father's best friend. Most important is the choosing of an intermediary whom they know the parents will not refuse.

The first step is for the intermediary to talk to the couple. After getting information about the situation, plans and wishes, the intermediary either calls up the parents or goes to the parents' home with the couple. Throughout the conversation between parents and intermediary, the couple remains silent. If this arrangement is not possible, the parents who are present take the intermediary role in settling the matter with the other parents. After discussing the situation, plans for the wedding will probably proceed. The usual philosophy is, "What else can we do except to allow them to get married?" Nevertheless, there are rare exceptions when the girl's parents take her back and do not agree to a wedding. Usually, however, even if the parents are angry, they do not refuse the supplications of the intermediary and the couple.

• *Job hunting*, or getting financial help. The Filipino considers it a great favor if someone can help him get employment. A lawyer's wife gave the following steps in the process by which a person from the province, or a godchild, seeks help.

(1) Those who are asking for help never go to a place or to a person without a preliminary gift (lubricant). They come to our place with fruits (mangoes) fresh from their farm. They select the best harvest of vegetables or rice, a chicken or other food. We can tell that a favor is going to be asked sooner or later.

(2) Small talk follows their arrival. Usually my husband asks the first question, "What can I do for you?" Normally, the relative or friend will not state immediately what he wants. His answer would be something like, "Oh, we just dropped by." Then my husband would pursue his first question, "Don't be shy. What can I help you with?" Then the person really feels that my husband means it, so he pours out his request.

(3) (Request stated.) He came to look for a job for his oldest son who just graduated from high school. The oldest son will not approach my husband directly so there are two intermediaries, or levels of intermediaries, involved by this time.

(4) (Assurance granted.) My husband will assure the man that he will try to keep his ears open about opportunities. He will promise to let them know as soon as possible.

The work is left to my husband. If he learns of an opening for a security guard in a textile mill, he will ask his friend, the chief of the security force, if he could have a place for his friend's son.

(6) My husband's friend will guarantee his help. He may have to go to some higher man in the company to get the job.

(7) (Period of waiting.) There will be occasional follow-up visits with gifts by the man asking for help.

(8) (Request granted.) It may take months, even years, before a job can be granted.

(9) (Gift giving by way of appreciation.) When the job has been granted, our friend or relative feels obliged to give us something in service or in kind. This process does not end with one gift but is carried on through life because

it is considered a big *utang na loob*. Whenever my husband visits these friends or relatives in the province, they treat him like a king. They feel more gratitude towards my husband than towards the person who hired the son. Sometimes this person is never even met or known. Gifts will also be extended to my husband's friend who worked out the details. These gifts will come from our friend or relative rather than from us.

In the process of hunting for a job, the intermediary has worked like a North American employment agency. There is a striking difference however. Instead of giving one payment for the service, the continual payment establishes and reinforces mutual obligation. This spreads a network of mutual obligation throughout the society and, in essence, provides the social cohesion needed to hold the society together, as well as the security an individual needs as part of that society.

• *Bearing unpleasant news* is done by a Filipino's intermediary. These opportunities include a death in the family, an elopement, failing to pass a board or bar exam, or seeing something unpleasant such as a slip showing beneath a skirt hemline, a hole in a boy's pants, or bad odor. Usually, if a girl sees a hole in a boy's pants, she looks for another boy who is his friend and asks him to tell the boy. The one telling the other will not inform him of who saw the hole first, avoiding undue embarrassment. If there is no fellow around, then the girl ignores it. Lovers and very close friends are exceptions to this type of practice. They can be more direct.

• *Making a complaint or a decision* is communicated through a middleman. If a complaint must come from a lower status person to a higher status one, a middleman is used, e.g., teacher to principal. In this case, the middleman would be the most experienced and influential teacher in the school.

When a decision has been made to lay off employees, the boss can approach an employee directly. On other occasions, the boss thinks it is better to have another person do it for him, for he feels the employee will take the news more calmly and maturely if it comes from a close friend.

Even in families, middlemen are used. If a child wants to ask his father for something, e.g., money for vacation, he will ask through the mother. If the mother wants to correct a younger daughter who will not take it graciously, she will ask the older daughter to do it. Because the sisters are good friends, the mother could utilize this route in getting her point across.

Not every request needs a middleman. It takes extra sensitivity to know. Each family differs in specific application but the principle remains the same.

76

• *Communicating indirectly to an adult: the reflector concept.* This involves the practice of talking to a child directly in an attempt to communicate indirectly to an adult. This concept is illustrated in the following case as related by a Filipino.

> An older lady visited our home with her son. We did not know what she wanted but she was the sister of a long-time friend of my parents. My mother got some information through talking with her, but most of it was disclosed through her conversation with her ten year old son—done intentionally to be heard by others.

The following conversation shows the message spoken and what was received by the parents.

Message verbalized: Son, we are really poor. We cannot go back to the province today. Maybe we have to stay here in town.
Message received: They want to stay for the night since they do not have any money.

Message verbalized: Son, Mr. and Mrs.— are so good to us. They are your uncle's friends.
Message received: She really apreciates the hospitality and kindness extended.

Message verbalized: Son, you see those sewing machines? Maybe if you learn to sew you can also earn some money.
Message received: She desires to have her child learn some skill so he will be able to work. It may be he will learn sewing.

Result: Both mother and son stayed with us for several days. The mother left the child with us. My mother gave the woman some money for her trip back to the province. The child helped with housework and errands for several months. He tried to learn to sew but did not enjoy it. Finally his mother came back for him.

• *Communicating with God.* The mediator practice makes Mariology a well accepted doctrine of the Roman Catholic Church. Mary is the mediator between God and man. It is easier for the Filipinos to identify with this system because they find it constantly practiced in their own society.

Qualifications of an intermediary
• He must be reachable, not too high on the status ladder, but high enough to exert natural influence, e.g. a godfather.
• He must have *malakas*, or a lot of "pull," and connections with the

right people. The expression, "It is not what you know but whom you know," holds good in the Philippines.

• He must be a capable person, one who has proven himself in his job and in the job of intermediary; for example, he has brought many conflicting persons together, or has helped a lot of unemployed friends and relatives.

Directness, frankness, or outspokenness are all contrary to the Filipino value of smooth interpersonal relations. Filipinos use go-betweens or reflectors to communicate. The political term that expresses this is "good offices" or mediator; the common term is intermediary (*padrino*); and the lover's term is "bridge."

The North American tends to take the direct approach, which is obnoxious to the Filipino, and is unable to accomplish all that he seeks to do. The role of the North American and his reputation could be enhanced if he became an effective mediator or intermediary. He would find that he was not only totally respected but that closed doors would swing open to him.

Notes and references

[1] Examples of the intermediary and the use of euphemistic or metaphorical language in the courtship and marriage situation may be found in F. Landa Jocano's *Growing up in a Philippine Barrio*. Holt, Rinehart and Winston, New York, 1969, 64–74.

Chapter 11

Conflict and Conflict Resolution

Conflict relationships

Filipinos place high values on smooth interpersonal relations (SIR).[1] As much as possible, a Filipino will avoid offending another or being offended himself. In spite of this, however, there are occasions when things get rough and snags develop in relationships. Examples include: (1) Younger children who will defy their older brothers and sisters who have authority over them. The oldest brother is sometimes more feared than the mother and father by the younger siblings; (2) The teacher who lays out his policies during the first day of class; when and if the student disregards these, there is conflict; and (3) The outsider who lives in keeping with his own sociocultural antecedents rather than adapting to the Filipino lifeway. The hurt inflicted in such situations is graded according to the intensity felt from mild to strong.

Offenses to the Filipino

• *Rude behavior* such as slamming the door in a person's face, answering back to parents or to older members of the family, or passing between two people talking without stooping down produces a mild form of reaction and a beginning conflict situation.

• *A breach of contract* such as not paying a large debt on the set date or not completing payment for property bought produces more than a mild reaction.

• *Personal insult* results from verbal combat when insults are uttered liberally. If no one is around to hear what is said, there is less hurt and therefore less potential conflict. But if other people witness the altercation, conflict is greater. It is a real shame to be put into such a

79

situation and it is a big scandal. This type of affront involves name calling and the humiliation of the opponent. For example:

A: You're rude, you're lewd; you're uneducated and without manners.

B: Be careful with your words. You don't know who you are talking to.

A: So what! Just because your father is the mayor you think you're already somebody.

B: Of course.

This type of altercation can go on indefinitely with each one degrading the other. When this type of insult comes from a family member or close friend, the wound is greater. The Filipino has the expression: "It was better for him to do physical hurt than to call and address me like that. A bruised head or broken arm can be healed, but the wounds caused by strong and incisive words will not be healed."

• *Ingratitude* or *walang utang na loob*, is ignoring a debt that comes from a deep sense of gratitude, and it hurts the Filipino intensely. There are different types of ingratitude.

(1) Elopement produces a deep hurt in the parents. Some respond by not talking to their children for a long period of time. Others do not allow the children to enter their home. If the couple are both still in school, then they must be prepared for the worst reception. However, the parents' hurt is less if the children have completed their studies.

The hurt caused by elopement can be healed, depending on the parents. Some parents forgive easily, others can but do not, and still others are utterly unable to forgive.

Elopement is considered to be an ungrateful act. The really angry parents would say, "You ingrate! After sending you to school this is what you give us in return." This is especially intense since the great pride of parents is to see their children finish college. Parents go to a lot of sacrifice and hard work to send their children to school, which increases the sense of indebtedness the children feel towards their parents. A college degree is a status symbol which raises the status of the whole family. Elopement definitely undermines the trust and respect of the parents.

Some couples try very hard to show that they are sorry and to ease the parents' hurt. Sometimes they succeed, but the best heart-melter is the grandchild. All hurt vanishes when the grandparents hear the cry of their newborn grandchild.

(2) School dropouts hurt the sponsor. An older brother or sister who educates a younger sibling expects him to educate another. A child who has been sent to school through the hardships of an older brother or sister has the responsibility to do the same for his younger brothers and sisters. The youngest member of the family enjoys most of the comforts of

life, although the responsibility of taking care of the parents may fall on him.

If the younger brother or sister drops out of school, the one supporting him is greatly hurt unless it is due to mental inability. Then the act is understood and forgiven. If the reason for dropping school were for marriage or irresponsibility, it would be difficult for the supporting siblings to forgive.

In one actual case, the younger sister eloped after an older sister had worked conscientiously to send her to nursing school. The elopement caused the older sister much grief, shame, and hurt, and she would not talk to her younger sister, the husband, or even to their baby. The whole family was divided over the incident. Though this is an extreme case, it is a good example of how the Filipino values gratefulness or *pagtanaw ng utang na loob*.

(3) Maligning hurts the benefactor. People who have been helped in finding a job consider this a big *utang na loob*. They show appreciation through gifts in kind or services. Hurt can result when the recipient of the help speaks against the benefactor. The benefactor expects the recipient to be good to him since he helped him and was good to him.

(4) Relatives or close friends who send a child to school expect to have the recipient remain a kind friend, and not say or do anything that shows ingratitude.

• *The unfaithful lover* produces an intense hurt, and a broken engagement is a wound that never heals. Since courting is a long and painful but rewarding process, engagement becomes an "oasis in a desert." If the engagement does not result in marriage, a great wound develops. However, if both the man and woman realize they would not get along, then the hurt is not so intense. But if the decision is unilateral, especially made by the man, the girl is likely to nurse a grudge to the grave. For example, if an engaged fellow were to leave his fiancée in the Philippines and fall in love with another woman while abroad, the Filipino girl at home would die of a broken heart. The girl's family would sympathize with her and hate the man. The hurt would never be forgiven and would be with bitterness.

• *A killing* is perhaps the most intense reason for hurt. In this case, no apology is attempted nor accepted. It will probably never be forgiven. If this happened in the provinces, the family involved would get revenge by killing a member of the offending family.

Concept of *nagtatanim*

Nagtatanim literally means "planting." It is an idiomatic expression which denotes that a person cannot forget or forgive a hurt. Instead of forgetting and forgiving the offender, the person offended nurses the hatred until it grows intense, then some kind of explosion is likely to follow. It is equivalent to "keeping a record of wrongs" or "nursing a grudge."

Signs of hurt

The Filipino is, generally, a very sensitive person in terms of the face-to-face encounter. He can easily sense if he is liked or disliked; he can accurately detect if a person is genuinely concerned; and he readily picks up clues to a person's anger. These clues cover the entire noise continuum from silence to loudness.

Whenever a Filipino bangs doors, rattles plates, or slams drawers, it is a pretty sure sign that he is angry. Though such activities are somewhat natural for the North American, they are not for the Filipino. During the normal course of events, the Filipino takes great pains to operate within the houshold silently. When a woman is angry it is said, "There she goes banging things."

On the other hand, when in the presence of someone of higher status, there is a tendency to withdraw into silence or to withdraw physically, both a part of the world of silence. For example:

One Filipino fellow was invited to eat with some Americans. The hostess was slightly late in preparing the meal. They finally ate about six thirty. After some time had elapsed, the Filipino said to the hostess, "I have to eat fast because I have to sing at a gathering at seven." The hostess responded, "Why didn't you say so sooner?"

The reason he did not say anything until the last minute was for fear that he would rush the hostess too much. However, a Filipino on good terms with an American would feel free to mention his appointment sooner.

In the same need for silence, a Filipino girl would not comment on her roommate's shabby way of dressing for fear that she would offend her. So she would keep quiet.

Resolution of conflict

The Filipino resolves conflict by means of two devices: action apology and through an intermediary.

Apology is a highly complex act. It varies with the offense. It involves both action as well as words. It is not enough to say, "I'm sorry," for words must be backed up by repentant action. Sometimes the verbal apology is not even needed if the actions suffice. One Filipino states:

In my family the phrase, "I'm sorry," is seldom heard. If I offend my mother, then communication is severed. Since I know I was wrong, I have the responsibility to initiate a conversation. Beginning the conversation is like saying, "I'm sorry." For example, I would say, "Mother, have you eaten?" If she simply responds "No," then I know she is still mad. I will try again. "What are we having for supper?" If she responds with more than just *"adobo"* (a basic Filipino dish), then I know she is opening up the channel of communication. The tone of her voice helps me know also what she is thinking. Without actually saying, "I'm sorry," the whole process of my opening the conversation communicates to her that I am accepting my fault and would like to renew our fellowship. Sometimes through this pacifier conversation I might ask whether she is still angry. A sweet smile flashes from her face which tells me, "Yes, I was but not anymore." Both parties are now at peace. The matter does not completely end there, however, for it may mean that I have to volunteer to wash the dishes and sweep the floor.

Washing dishes does not always mean that one person is being punished or that he just kindheartedly volunteered. It may also mean someone is trying to appease an angry father or mother. Appeasement is always done through good works which parents will accept.[2]

The same holds true for brothers and sisters. Silence, which may last for hours, follows a fight. The first one who initiates the conversation shows he is sorry and wants a truce. The whole pacifying process sometimes takes a day, depending on the cause of the fight.

Action apology may need to be accompanied by the use of an intermediary. In the case where children fight and fail to resolve their differences after a period of time, the father or mother must step in to mediate. The process of mediation depends on the specific family involved. A girl gives the following example:

When my father mediated between my sister and me, he would call both of us and let us stand in front of him. Then he would ask my sister and me questions regarding our misunderstanding. After hearing both sides of the conflict he would say, "As the older one, you should give in," and "As the younger one you should learn to respect your sister." Then he would ask us to shake hands.

The whole process of resolution of hurt caused by rude behavior, personal insult, or petty misunderstanding goes something like this: (1) explosion; (2) silence; (3) pacification, first by the initiation of conversation, and then by the use of mediators, be it mother, father, older siblings, relatives, or friend; and (4) supporting actions which ultimately lead to further interaction. At times one and two both occur; at other times either the explosion or silence is sufficient to bring in the need for a mediator.

In the instances of the unfaithful lover or a killing, no apology can be made. Following World War II, all the Filipinos hated the Japanese. Just the mention of "Japanese" or *saking* (bow-legged) made them furious. Some Filipinos still hate the Japanese who massacred Filipino children, civilians, and soldiers, but now they tend to separate the Japanese of World War II from the Japanese of the present time. Although there are still some who nurse that hatred, they are the exception, not the rule.

Cases of accidental killing produce less intense feelings than outright murder, such as a driver running over a child or hitting an elderly man or woman. To prevent charges from being pressed against him, the driver looks for someone to be his advocate.[3] This could be his parent or godparents. The intermediary should know the victim or someone who knows somebody who knows the victim. By this means, he can exert the right influence and pull the right strings. If the victim is lower status than the driver, an intermediary is not needed. The higher status driver can do the influencing himself. This tends to produce an injustice causing the lower status person to receive unjust treatment. There are other cases, though, where the lower status person takes advantage of his misfortune and asks for more money from the driver, since he obviously is a wealthy man and can afford a large sum of money.

The driver through the good help of a mediator receives a lesser penalty. Instead of appearing in court and paying a lawyer, for example, he may only pay the hospital bill and give some money to the family. Thus, the mediator pleads or talks the victim into agreeing with the settlement.

Apology, then, in the Philippine context is more than words. It also involves true evidence of being sorry through actions. Such actions frequently need to be sustained until the offender knows that he has been completely forgiven. These actions involve gifts, services, and good works in keeping with the expectations of reciprocity.

How to administer a rebuke

The property custodian forgot to lock the windows of the church every night. The pastor seeks to correct him:

Rev. Nebab: Hello, Ben. How are you?
Benjie: Fine, Pastor.
Rev. Nebab: Have you enrolled at the night school yet?
Benjie: Yes, Pastor. I enrolled yesterday.
Rev. Nebab: Good. Are you enjoying your work here at the church?
Benjie: Yes, Pastor.
Rev. Nebab: Good, I was afraid you were not enjoying it.
Benjie: What made you say that, Pastor?

84

Rev. Nebab: Well, it's really not me, Benjie. I am thinking about the executive committee. You know how strict they are, especially Mr. Filario. You know the things inside the church building are all expensive and we don't want them stolen. For three Sundays now you have forgotten to lock the windows. But I know you meant to lock them, only you were, perhaps, in a hurry to go somewhere. I understand how hard it is to be a student and working as well. I used to do both myself.

Benjie: Thank you, Pastor, for your understanding. I will lock the windows from now on.

Rev. Nebab: Good. By the way, how many subjects are you going to take this semester?

Benjie: Six subjects, Pastor.

Rev. Nebab: What are they?

Benjie: Accounting, Spanish, English and three others. I don't recall offhand.

Rev. Nebab: Good. How is your girlfriend?

Benjie: Just fine, Pastor. We did have a misunderstanding the other day so we are not back on speaking terms yet.

Rev. Nebab: Oh! Why?

Benjie: Well, because I wanted to sit by her in church but she didn't want me to because she was afraid her father would scold her. But I sat with her anyway.

Rev. Nebab: Well, go and ask for her forgiveness so you will be reconciled.

Benjie: Yes, Pastor.

Rev. Nebab: Well, I'll be going now, Benjie.

Benjie: Bye, Pastor.

From now on Benjie will make sure that he locks the windows. He would not want to hurt Rev. Nebab, disappoint him, or put him in a bad light in relation to the executive committee. While Pastor Nebab was explaining, he noticed tension building on the part of Benjie so he quickly changed the subject, and after his brief visit, departed.

Notes and references

[1] For further discussion of SIR, see Frank Lynch. "Social Acceptance Reconsidered," in *Four Readings on Philippine Values*. IPC Papers, No. 2, Ateneo de Manila University Press, Quezon City, 1968, 1–63.

[2] The family practice of appeasement carries over into the religious realm where the Filipino continues to appease God with good works. In this regard, see also Vitaliano R.

Gorospe. "Christian Renewal of Filipino Values," in *Split-Level Christianity (and) Christian Renewal of Filipino Values*. Ateneo University Press, Quezon City, 1966, 19–59.

[3] A law in the Philippines, similar to other Spanish countries, states that the driver of a vehicle is always guilty in such accidental deaths.

Chapter 12

Celebration

Hosting a dinner out

In developing loyalty to a person or group, special events are necessary. Celebrations are one characteristic means of gaining or rewarding the loyalty of others in the Philippines. They may take place in the home, the church, the local restaurant, or in a nearby city (probably in a restaurant).

In the United States, a list of guests is carefully made and those who arrive at the event are screened for admission. If anyone enters because of careless security, (i.e., an open door), or is invited by a friend, he falls into the category of a freeloader and is made to feel unwanted. There are certain exceptions to this rule. For instance, some weddings and receptions give an open invitation and it is expected that friends of the bride or groom will participate. As a general rule, those interested in the couple attend and those not interested do not attend.

In the Philippines, the list is only a starting point. The hostess doubles quantities in order to have enough. If there is to be a private dinner planned for eight, ten might show up. If the dinner is for one hundred, two hundred might arrive. The American hostess who has each quantity carefully measured in keeping with the number invited is nonplussed. Her concern is how a roast for eight will stretch to serve ten. The Filipino hostess, on the other hand, is flattered that two more uninvited guests have arrived to make the celebration more significant. The food will always go around since extra was prepared. If extra people do not come, there is a sense of failure in that the event was not seen as worthy of people's time and energy.

No one "crashing the party" is considered to be irresponsible in the traditional Filipino community, though there is a sense of gatecrashing and freeloading developing in the new emerging Filipino lifeway. Basically, the extra person is welcomed and made to feel as one of the party.

When the Filipino receives an unexpected gift, bonus, or windfall, he will probably take his best friends (his alliance) to the restaurant. In this case, the invitation list is limited, though there might be an extra one or two in a large dinner party. The host will pick out a restaurant he can afford and will always figure restaurant, size of party, cost of entrée and extras so that he can say, "The sky is the limit," and have sufficient funds to cover all expenses. He will pay cash and the money will change hands with the proprietor of the restaurant to cover all the obligations so that the host will not lose face. Only the very highest status Filipinos will pay by check since checking accounts are limited in number.

The Filipino host makes all decisions for the guests—what to order, how much, and when it will be served. He may let the guests make the selection but he will encourage a more expensive entrée, a choice of speciality to go along with the main dinner, and an addition here or there, until he has made sure everyone not only has the most expensive and impressive selection but also will leave the party with a good taste in his mouth and an emotional satisfaction. Even if the guest does not like the particular entrée the host has selected or urged upon him, he still likes the process.

The North American, on the other hand, even though he also makes the selection of restaurant, will operate quite differently as host. He might say, "Order what you like," but what he means is, order in keeping with his financial condition, the nature of the dinner party, and other factors of good taste. He might also give the guests a clue as to what he will order, but he tries to let each guest select his own entrée without too much external coercion. If the host is too definitive in his urging, whether or not the guests like the actual food served them, they will feel shortchanged in the experience if they are not free to choose what they want. This is carried to such an extreme in American society that when an organizational dinner is planned at a restaurant with a special price arrangement, at least two entrées are permitted to allow the American choice.

If the Filipino is left in doubt as to the amount of food to order or the price range from which to select, he is uncomfortable if not actually embarrassed. The dinner is not the success that he had anticipated and he goes away feeling that the host lacks not only social graces but intelligence as well.

Whereas the American plunges into the meal without giving much thought to which utensils to use, how to use them and what order of foods to eat, the Filipino pays a great deal of attention to each of these details and many more. Any observed deviation from the pattern produces embarrassment which may spoil the experience. The North American cannot be too thorough in communicating effectively the various cues of behavior to the Filipino in his home or setting; nor can the American be too careful in his participation within the Filipino setting.

One of the main conflicts in order of eating between the two cultures is in the use of the beverage. The American may drink his beverage prior to the meal and continue drinking throughout the meal. The Filipino ends his meal with a beverage. He will not eat any solids after he has had his beverage. This holds true when eating a meal or when serving refreshments. The order is firmly fixed: solids then beverage. In fact, only one cup of tea or coffee is served at the close of a meal. The average American, having to wait throughout the meal for his beverage, is likely to desire an extra cup, and will indicate his wish. Asking for and receiving a second cup from a gracious hostess is in very poor taste.

Banquets or dinner parties are frequently delayed until the person of highest status is present. This becomes a hardship when the person seeking to reinforce his high standing in a community group delays for hours. Banquet guests have sometimes waited two to three hours for the honored or high status guest who needs no excuse for being tardy. For the American this creates two hardships: one is having to wait long past his expected time to eat; the other is to eat food that has become cold.

Hospitality

When the Filipino drops in on a friend or relative, he is treated graciously and will be served refreshments in keeping with his status— coke, beer, or champagne for high status people; coffee or tea for low status. The average Filipino will have the water on and off the fire all day long in anticipation of the unexpected guest. If the guest is in the home at mealtime, he is cordially invited to partake.

The North American readily offends the Filipino at this point for he sees the home as a closed place, open only to his family (nuclear) and invited guests. Even if the home is more open than that of most North Americans, the table is still usually closed to others. Meals are family occasions unless special preparation has been made for a specific invitation occasion. The Filipino may frequently be asked to join the table at mealtime, but the invitation is only given once. The Filipino will refuse that first invitation even though he has not eaten. Since the American frequently does not extend a second invitation, the Filipino is left alone in the living room with a cookie in his hand, finally urged upon him by the hostess. He is disappointed as well as alienated since he wanted the food, the fellowship, and the opportunity to satisfy his curiosity as to what the American eats.

The Filipino entering a friend's home spends time just visiting and catching up on things first. He does not let business intrude in this preliminary period. To do so would be rude and would insure a negative response from his hosts. This period of friendly interchange may last an hour. It is only when refreshments are brought and finished that business matters are discussed. Throughout the preliminary period, feelers are extended to check out the climate in which the request is to be made. If the favor seeker senses that the climate is favorable to his request, he will make it. If, however, he feels the climate is not favorable, he will leave without giving any indication of what the request was.

The American wants to get right down to business. He has more important things to do than sitting around chatting. He may not serve refreshments at all. Finally, he may blurt out his request if he is the favor seeker, or call on the guest to state his favor if he is the host. Any of these practices are disruptive of the smooth interpersonal relationships sought by the Filipino. The Filipino goes away embarrassed, chagrined, and disappointed; the American is irritated and frustrated.

Chapter 13

A Value Profile

A basic values taxonomy

Values are whatever an individual or group considers to be important; some values are more basic than others. In each automatic or consciously-made decision some value underlies the choice. Every group, culture, or subculture has its own pattern or network of values. These values are what make each community unique; they cause a community to grow and to maintain interest in life. Without them, life becomes humdrum, boring, and dull.

Basic values underlie all other value patternings, and they permit the one seeking to understand a society the ability to describe the society by means of the basic values taxonomy.[1] The taxonomy can be utilized in a number of ways, but for the purpose of a description of the value orientation of the Filipino, discussion will follow a simple listing of the values within the overall profile. The basic values needed to describe the Filipino society include: (1) vulnerability seen as a weakness, (2) personalness, (3) event orientation, (4) prestige is ascribed, (5) focused authority, (6) multialternatives, and (7) holism. Because of the expression of these values, others such as linearity and time orientation become integral parts of the values profile.

The contribution of the basic values taxonomy lies in its ability to anticipate conflict caused from a difference of values. The profile acts as a radar, seeking out potential areas of conflict and suggesting ways and means of resolving that conflict without taking personal affront.[2]

Application of the profile to the Filipino

• *Vulnerability is seen as a weakness.* In certain circumstances, the Filipino appears to value vulnerability as a strength and readily admits to things the North American never would. These include an illicit sexual involvement, matters relating to one's personal toilet, and reference to gas, menstrual period, and urinating. However, through most of his life the Filipino is very sensitive to vulnerability—any evidence of weakness, of erring, of mistake, or of accident. The individual and society as a corporate body work together to cover all evidence of weakness.

When someone stumbles, falls, or harms himself in any way, Filipinos will stand and laugh rather than help the injured person. To the North American, this appears to be crass insensitivity and an unwillingness to become involved. But the Filipino sees it differently. To stumble is to show weakness. To respond to this seriously would underscore and bring attention to the weakness, producing embarrassment. Ultimately, especially if great harm has been done, the injured person would be obligated to reciprocate the assistance. Paying attention to one stumbling communicates, "Why are you so clumsy?" rather than, "I'm interested in helping you."

A group of Filipinos in an automobile traveling to Manila came upon the scene of an accident. A policeman forced them to stop and asked that one of the accident victims be taken to Manila. At first the request was refused. The policeman drew his pistol and made them take the accident victim. Because they were forced to help by the use of a pistol, they were released from the onus of involvement, and the victim would not be obligated or embarrassed. Had they taken the victim voluntarily, they would have been underscoring the weakness.

Losing is an evidence of weakness. An athletic team, or any member of the team, will give all the excuses possible for losing the game in order to save face. The game might even end in a brawl if victory is not in sight. In politics, a candidate almost always conceives a scheme to assure his winning. If he does not succeed, he demands a recounting of ballots or makes his appeal to the highest tribunal. This is especially true if he is the incumbent, for with the appeal on the books, he might get to hold on to his office until the next election. In school or church elections, unless the winners are part of larger alliances, they do not expect to get the cooperation of the losers and their followers.

A great deal of covering up is done in politics to safeguard one's reputation. Criticisms are ignored rather than considered and evaluated. Defensiveness shows up when one is interviewed on television or for a newspaper article. Seldom does a politician admit to mistake or error. If he did, he would be vulnerable and people would not trust him anymore.[3]

A fellow courting a girl of higher status than he will try hard to impress her. Poverty is considered a weakness, so if he is poor he does not let the girl know it.[4] He will dress well, take her to expensive places and even rent a car when he goes to see her. (Cars are the privilege of the few. Those who belong to the lower status will avoid embarrassment by not even thinking of courting a girl of high status.)

The Filipino seeks to have smooth interpersonal relationships in every encounter. He wants no friction or crisis that will estrange, alienate, or disrupt these relationships. Filipinos cannot disagree openly. They cover up any disruption or upset as much as possible.

Pakikisama, or smooth companionship, is the operating factor among those who really want to remain friends. Note the following:

> Pedro has an examination the next day but his friends, Oscar and Pablo, invite him to see a movie. For the sake of *pakikisama*, Pedro goes along and forgets about the exam.

. . . .

> Linda has fifty pesos to pay for her room and board the following day, but her friend Perla needs money for some reason. Linda lends her the money for *pakikisama*, although she does not have any idea when she will be repaid. As for her landlady, she says, "Let God take care of it. Whatever will be, will be."

Another mark of the Filipino's vulnerability or desire to keep the vulnerability from showing is the means used to appear strong. Using an intermediary when asking a favor eliminates the possibility of facing a negative answer. He will also make an effort to have companionship at all times. When death occurs, relatives come from everywhere to be with the family of the deceased. The whole family will remain for days with the patient in the hospital. Children are not left alone at night. Even a guest is never out of sight or call of some member of the household.[5] An adequate excuse for not attending an event is, "I didn't have a companion."

The North American also considers vulnerability as a weakness, but his pattern of responding is different. Any questioning of his ability, for example, makes him vulnerable and causes him to express the behavior of vulnerability as a weakness. Further, his society does not stand behind him in this value orientation as much as the Filipino society does. The Filipino society provides its members with many social mechanisms to cover their weaknesses.

• *Personalness is highly valued.* The North American adult society is personal to the degree that its members encourage the larger good for the individual. The entire system of American society is designed to let the individual have all he needs for a good life personally. Certain North American youth subcultures have seen this as being impersonal, for face-to-face awareness and sensitivity is that which is involved in personalness for them. The Filipino combines both approaches, though the latter is by far the most influential. Face-to-face personalness, being aware of all the nonverbal cues to attitudes and responses of people, has been developed to a fine art by the Filipino. To maintain those smooth interpersonal relationships that are so important to him, he begins with the face-to-face encounter. Whatever else works out is fine. The broader factors of personal need and fulfillment always yield to the immediacy of the personal encounter.

Personal support of others is expressed through tactile, or touch behavior, indicating not only a dependence one upon another but also communicating something very personal and individual. A man will hold a man's hand as a sign of respect and trust; members of the same sex will lay a hand on the other's knee; a person will touch another in a crowd. A woman will put an arm around another woman, pinch or pat another at greeting, or even pat the stomach of a pregnant woman. This value extends to the nontouch but supportive behavior insisting that no one be alone, enjoying the presence of another, or at least the symbol of their presence, as a light on in the dark. Relatives come and stay just to provide company.

The Filipino likes a personality figure, one who relates warmly to him and makes him feel he is a person and is important. This person will build a network of interpersonal obligations with many others through the expression of his interest and needs.

The face-to-face sensitivity of the Filipino expresses itself also in the use of euphemism.[6] For example, rather than say "no" to someone who wants to borrow an umbrella that the owner does not want to loan, he may say, "I don't think it is going to rain." No Filipino will take offense to this reply.

Interest in the person extends beyond the face-to-face encounter, especially in the family and extensions of the family through close and enduring friendships. In the United States, the Jack Brickhouse type of radio and television announcer is rare, i.e., one who relates personally to the team members and who incorporates this personal information and interest into the broadcast in which he is participating. But in the Philippines, rather than being the exception, it is the rule that the announcer be involved in the lives of one or more players and that he let this be known. In fact, it is possible to listen to a game for a long period without being told the score, for the announcer is too busy relating personal anecdotes. Filipinos relate very personal and intimate experiences in public.

The North American, by comparison, is impersonal in interpersonal relationships, has a patent insensitivity to others, and has a particular distaste for the personality type. He is formal, closed, and will attempt by various means to make the personality just one more of the crowd and relate to the whole group equally.

• *Event orientation*. In nearly every experience of life the Filipino is more concerned with the event itself and what is going on, than in when the event begins, ends, or if it moves within a narrow time schedule. He is unlike the North American who pays close attention to the narrow-grained time units of the second, minute, and hour, thus limiting the event. The Filipino lets the event evolve; timing is secondary. This expresses itself in a variety of ways. If something does not get done today, he excuses it by talking about *mañana* or tomorrow. His livelihood is built around an event so that if he can make a living by selling one item, he does not need to be in the office from eight to five. If something interferes with his plans or schedule, he patiently endures. If a social event was scheduled to end at ten o'clock—and it was still going—there would not be the strain to bring it to a close, nor would there be the irritation because it was continuing which would characterize a North American gathering. Few make appointments with professional people. When one is sick he just goes to the doctor; if his tooth hurts he goes to the dentist's office and waits until he can be cared for.

To a degree, there is change within the urban setting. Less focus is on the event and more attention is given to the clock-controlled time schedule. Nevertheless, this development comes slowly and still excludes many experiences of life.

The Filipino is a "now" person who concentrates on the moment and what it yields rather than looking to yesterday or tomorrow. He is very good at starting something and not continuing it later. Some speak of this as *ningas kogon*, something started with real zest and then waning enthusiasm.

The event orientation value makes the Filipino the master of time instead of its slave. It helps him be flexible, sometimes too flexible. He may not always get the job done on time but he finds enjoyment in the process of doing it. This leaves the North American frustrated. He considers the Filipino irresponsible and lazy; whereas, actually, he is responsible and energetic within his own distinct system of social interaction.

The Filipino has a schedule, though not in keeping with time. The American sets up a time schedule. He starts at a certain time, moves through specific timed units, and ends at a certain time. The Filipino moves from one event to another. When one event is finished—whatever the time is—he will move to the next event. He is finished when the list of activities or events is completed. He may go to his office at a certain time and open it, but if the work he has lined up is finished, he will close the office and go on to the next thing he had planned. The North American keeps his office open whether he has any business or not.

The Filipino is also punctual within the event schedule. North Americans are irked by Filipinos coming late for appointments, thinking the Filipino has no concept of time. But, for the Filipino, since event is more important than time, a person can be tied up in an event and ignore the next time period and appointment. Punctuality is more closely tied in with status than the clock. The lower one's status, the greater attention he pays to punctuality; the higher his status, the less attention he pays to punctuality. The higher status person simply must arrive at an event after the lower status people in order to maintain his higher standing. If the person calling the event is a high status person, the range of punctuality permitted others is very narrow. If the person calling the event is lower status than some attending, then the event will start in keeping with the attendance of the group as directed by status expectations. The following chart provides guidelines for such responses (see figure 9).

• *Prestige is ascribed.* One's prestige and standing in the community is acquired at birth. He starts at the level of the family status, though higher status can be achieved through education, marriage, or luck. Frequently, the motivation for education is not to acquire knowledge but to get a diploma which may bring a higher status level. A person's family name causes those associated with the family to expect good of him and to expect that he will succeed in either maintaining or improving the status of the family.

• *Focused authority.* Filipinos have a high view of authority. Anyone in authority is given due respect, evidenced by the soft-spokenness when in the presence of the authority figure. Such differential behavior is accorded one's boss, employer, professors and teachers, government officials, parents, and older siblings.

In school, the teacher is clearly the authority. Students know this and are expected to behave accordingly. Generally, everything the teacher says is taken as being truth because he is expected to master his subject. The teacher, on the other hand, knows his position and safeguards it from any attempts to undermine it.

The employer is the authority in the office. What the employer says goes, and any disagreement with him is avoided. Employees are expected to respect both his office and his person.

At home, the parents are the authorities. Respect and obedience to parents are highly valued. Because of this, Filipinos find it hard to tolerate what some American children "get away with" with their

PERSON	Social Event	Business Meeting	Church Activity	Appointment	EVENT
VIP (government) officials, business executives, visitors)	on time	on time	on time	on time	VIP's can come late, in fact it is almost expected.
Businessmen	15-30 minutes (range of punctuality)	on time		on time	
Professor Teacher	15-30 minutes (range of punctuality)	on time		on time	
Friends	15 minutes-1 hour (range of punctuality)		15-30 minutes	15-30 minutes	

Figure 9. **Punctuality**

parents. An American son might say to his father, "You don't know what you are doing," or, "You're chicken!" (perhaps in a teasing way). Or he might say, "Shut up!" These words are forbidden to children in the Philippines when talking to their parents. The position of the parents is "holy ground." They are never talked to as equals but always as parents. Filipinos think American children are ill-mannered and disrespectful. The Americans, however, think the Filipino child cannot speak and think for himself because he will not disagree openly or argue with people in authority.

Older brothers and sisters are viewed as authority figures by the younger members of the family. Age and authority go together. Whenever there are disagreements in a Filipino family, the younger is supposed to give in because he is younger. The Filipino younger member of the family may have truth but his voice may not be heard.

• *Multialternatives*. The Filipino attempts to avoid crises which would disrupt smooth interpersonal relations. Instead, he follows every possible avenue to "feel someone out" before taking a stand, making a request, or extending a favor. For example, the practice of using an intermediary to protect someone from the force of a "no" answer avoids crises.

The parent will not want to make a scene, so he will pursue whatever course is necessary to appease his child. This appears to be highly permissive to the American. However, this does not mean that the child grows up to be immature in his adult behavior, for at a certain point in his development the Filipino exercises mature behavior in spite of the more permissive early training.

The Filipino seeks out numerous signs that someone would be willing to be a godparent or sponsor to his child before he takes action. He also considers many possibilities before selecting someone to represent him or before he settles on a specific course of action in time of need.[7] This deliberateness is seldom shown on the surface of life. It is necessary to get into the intimate group before one can fully appreciate what goes on before any action is taken.

• *Holism* is understood as it is manifested in action as in a behavioral science explanation of the Manila traffic pattern.

The Filipino is holistic not particularistic. He thus sees the traffic situation as a whole and every part within the whole, whereas the North American can isolate one part and consider it.

The Filipino is holistic and nonlinear, not sequential and linear; he sees the pattern as flow, not as lanes of traffic. If there is space for him to go around on the shoulder or in the oncoming lane, he will. He will do this whatever the consequences of blocking traffic.

The Filipino is a noncrisis person. He knows what is going on around him and moves very cautiously when changing position. He progressively sounds out his move to make sure he can accomplish it. A horn blast will tell him to stay where he is, otherwise he will move out. Once he has his "nose" out in front of another, he has the right of way (see trust-humiliation). Any attempt to thwart him at this point or to reprimand him later will humiliate him and make him angry. He never wants to make a scene. Even when he "blows his stack" he is tremendously embarrassed but feels he has no control because of the great humiliation involved.

Vulnerability is a weakness to a Filipino, not a strength. He never looks at the other driver when he is making a traffic maneuver. If he were to do so, he would be calling attention to the other's vulnerability or admitting his own, depending on whether he achieved his right of way or failed to gain it. If he is ever in an accident he will not aid the persons injured since any such aid would clearly indicate or underscore the other person's vulnerability. He is sure the other person would not want his own weakness pointed up in this way.

He is event oriented, not time oriented, so if he bogs down in traffic he will accept it somewhat stoically.[8]

Notes and references

[1] For further details of the basic values taxonomy, see Marvin K. Mayers, *Christianity Confronts Culture*. Zondervan, Grand Rapids, Michigan, 1974.

[2] For alternative approaches to the study of Filipino values and behavior patterns, see:

Jaime Bulatao. "The Manileño's Mainsprings," in *Four Readings on Philippine Values*. Third edition, revised and enlarged. Frank Lynch and Alfonso de Guzman II, Editors, IPC Papers No. 2, Ateneo de Manila University Press, Quezon City, 1970, 89–114.

Felicidad V. Cordero and Isabel S. Panopio. "Contemporary Philippine Values," in *General Sociology: Focus on the Philippines*. College Professors Publishing Corporation, Manila, 1968.

George M. Guthrie and Fortunata M. Azores. "Philippine Interpersonal Behavior Patterns," in *Modernization: Its Impact in the Philippines III*. IPC Papers, No. 6. Ateneo de Manila University Press, Quezon City, 1968, 3–63.

[3] As Theodore Friend has stated it: "To criticize (political) opponents publicly (is) a serious matter for the job or role of that person (is) not separated from his personal, his familial, and even broader consideration of face." Theodore Friend. *Between Two Empires*. Yale University Press, New Haven, 1965, 29.

[4] In the play entitled "A Portrait of the Artist as Filipino" by Nick Joaquin, two of the characters panicked when the lights in the house went out, fearing it was because the bill had not been paid by their relatives. They said, "How could they possibly allow us to suffer this horrible, horrible humiliation! The neighbors will be there at the windows pointing and laughing and jeering." Nick Joaquin. "A Portrait of the Artist as Filipino,"

in *New Writing from the Philippines*. Edited by Leonard Casper. Syracuse University Press, Syracuse, 1966, 334–335.

[5] For additional insights regarding this Filipino value, see Elisa M. Espineli. *Offending the Filipino without even Trying*, m.s. A creative project offered the Wheaton Graduate School, Wheaton, Illinois, 1972.

[6] For further discussion of euphemisms, see Frank Lynch. "Social Acceptance Reconsidered," in *Four Readings on Philippine Values*. IPC Papers, No. 2. Ateneo de Manila University Press, Quezon City, 1968, 10–12.

[7] As an illustration of seeking multialternatives, consider this description of Manuel Quezon, past President of the Philippines. "Quezon liked to breed alternatives in the same way a horticulturist grows roses—in hopes that one will win a prize." Theodore Friend. *Between Two Empires*. Yale University Press, New Haven, 1965, 140.

[8] For an alternative analysis of the Manila traffic pattern, see R. L. Stone. "Private Transitory Ownership of Public Property: One Key to Understanding Public Behavior: I—The Driving Game," in *Modernization: Its Impact in the Philippines*. IPC Papers, No. 4. Ateneo de Manila University Press, Quezon City, 1967, 53–63.

Chapter 14

Education

Problems in contemporary Filipino education

Education to be maximally effective should be responsive to and serve the needs of the community to be educated. It should further fit the structure of the community so there will be a positive response toward the educational process and its results, as for example, "I really needed this," or "This has helped me," or "It was worth the effort."

Further, education should prepare members of the community for effective contact beyond the bounds of the community. It can provide some degree of composure as one moves back and forth across cultural and subcultural boundaries. It is the uneducated who might fear contact with the outside world; the educated need have no such fear.

Generally speaking, education motivated within a given community has been responsive to its community needs. However, such education is severely limited as to quality and quantity. To find educational opportunities beyond the lower levels of education a student moves out into the larger Filipino world and even to other nations such as China and the United States.

Two processes have thus dominated Filipino education. First, progressive change in the Philippines has centered in Manila (see figure 10) with only fine threads of influence extending into the provincial areas. This has resulted in very little progress outside of Manila. The bulk of the Philippines has been left untouched. Secondly, the majority of Filipinos have suffered from this process since most of those who were progressive in the provinces ultimately went to Manila, creating a "brain drain" from the provinces.[1] Further, some of the finest minds of the Philippines have

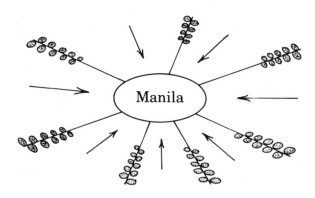

Key: ◉◉◉◉◉◉ those able to cling to strands
      ——————— strands of progress ————▸ "brain drain"

Figure 10. **Manila Development**

been siphoned off to Hong Kong and other areas surrounding the Philippines and also to the United States.

Unfortunately for the Philippines, two processes begin to operate, neither of which advances the Filipino lifeway nor serves the Filipino caught in the movement away from his or her local area. The one seeking the progressive opportunity through education beyond the local community is in the new educational setting long enough to become enculturated somewhat into the new lifestyle and is reluctant to return to the source area. The Filipino thus disassociated from his past speaks glowingly and proudly of his source area but also expresses his distaste for any consideration of returning permanently.

As stated above, the Filipino is only enculturated in part to the new lifestyle and never fully adapts to it. More significantly, he is never fully accepted into the new setting. Schoolteachers or pastors, for example, assigned away from their source area find themselves in tension between the demands of the new setting and a kind of homesickness drawing them to the home of their parents. This is felt most strongly by the wife.[2] Such tension limits their effective ministry.

One reaction to reverse the brain drain is to hold back those that might be drained off by giving them limited opportunity to advance. However, to deprive people of opportunities to progress, and thus to prosper, not only slows down progress everywhere but also produces bitterness on the part of those held back. This bitterness can be forcefully directed at those perceived as depriving the Filipinos of opportunities.

The inadequacy of imported educational programs

Education motivated from outside the Philippines has generally been marginally responsive to the local and national community. Rather, it encourages business practices which fit the outsider's own social structures. Missions enter with the goal of missionizing through education and their schools reflect their own goals of pastoral training and Bible study. The end result of such business and religious preparation is frequently a displaced Filipino striving for additional education and preparation in the source nation of the business or mission.

The Filipino educator, along with the guest educator, may profit from the overview of Filipino social structure, social relations and value orientation presented in the first part of this book. Further, they may also profit from insights available to the educator as he applies such understandings to the task of education in the Philippines.

General principles applicable to Philippine education

• *Education should be an extension of the alliance.*

(1) Other options seen as inadequate are that the alliance become the extension of the school, but this could reverse the normal socialization process inherent in the society; or that both continue going their own ways, which would maintain the discontinuity between the two.

(2) Each alliance or alignment of alliances needs its own school. Since the alliance is the focus for security and loyalty development, any school outside the alliance would tend to produce insecurity potential and would divide loyalties.

(3) The leader of the alliance or alignment of alliances should be responsible for the education of each child within the alliance, arranging for the location and personnel of the school. A national regulatory board should be formed composed of high status heads of alliances as well as representative heads of alliances from all the statuses. In effect, each head of an alignment or alliance should serve on this regulatory board.

(4) Local autonomy over the educational process could result in provincialism. Teacher's colleges might guard against this possibility if all teachers were required to attend one. Full time personnel, required to attend short term institutes in the Manila colleges and universities, would staff the teacher's colleges and be available as visiting staff of the Manila schools.

(5) A system of diplomas should be established for teachers in each level of progress in this system. The diploma, an external motivation needed to achieve development of learning, should carry with it the possibility of increased wages and/or higher status. Without it, the teacher might not feel the need for further schooling.

• *Education should be status oriented.*

(1) Status people should be responsible for the school, either teaching it or administering it. The highest status person in the organization of the community should be continually involved, however superficially, in the educational program.

(2) Educational achievement should be recognized as one of the present criteria for receiving increased respect through the status system.

(3) All local schools should relate to Manila schools in a status relationship. Every school system needs local extensions as well as a Manila-based school for status reasons.

(4) Every student educated at any level of status throughout the educational system must be given an opportunity to attend a Manila school, if only for a short time, as a capstone to his educational career. Multistatus schools need to be provided to educate people from all statuses.

• *Local education should be upgraded in order to minimize brain drain.*

(1) Young people assigned to any locale to teach or engage in other activities should spend from three to five years gaining the trust of the people.

(2) Schools placed strategically in first class cities as extensions of the Manila school, and schools placed strategically in smaller cities of from two to five in rank as extensions of the Manila school or the first class city school, would allow the young person to continue to maintain ties with his local community (see figure 11). They may also help him either to resist the urge to study abroad, or if he does travel, to continue stronger ties with his local area than would be otherwise possible.

A specific approach

• *The university with its extensions.* The foundation for this plan is to have an educational program involving institutions on two separate status levels within the society (see figure 12). The institution with the highest status—offering the highest degree, accepting only B.A. students from accredited colleges and universities and demanding the highest financial cost—would be the university. It would have primarily two divisions: specialization and communications.

The university could operate independently or in conjunction with a status college or university in the rural community. At least three extensions of it should be established in key first class cities.

The purpose of the extensions would be three-fold:

(1) To extend quality education beyond Manila;

(2) To have the highest status base possible for members of the teaching staff who can then be professors in a status university and still

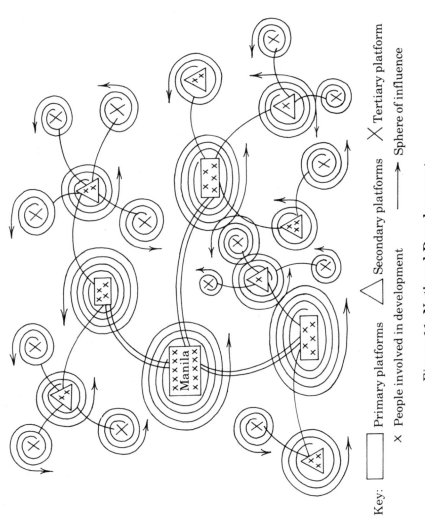

Key:
▭ Primary platforms △ Secondary platforms ✕ Tertiary platform

✕ People involved in development ⟶ Sphere of influence

Figure 11. **National Development**

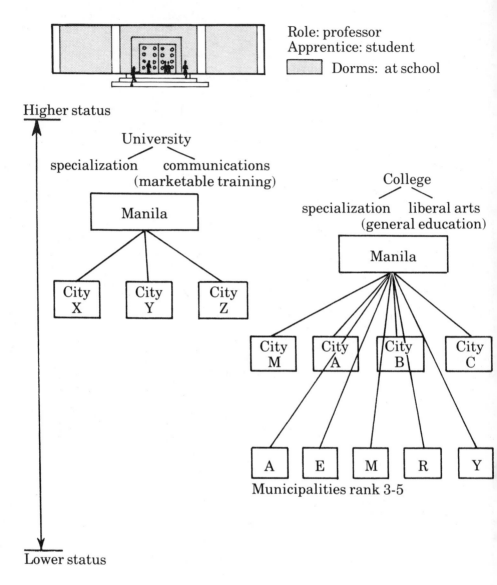

Role: professor
Apprentice: student
Dorms: at school

Higher status

University
specialization   communications
(marketable training)

Manila

City X   City Y   City Z

College
specialization   liberal arts
(general education)

Manila

City M   City A   City B   City C

A   E   M   R   Y
Municipalities rank 3-5

Lower status

Key:. City ⟶ full program (English)
Municipality ⟶ partial program (English + trade language)

Figure 12. **Educational Plan**

move into the provincial area to carry on a program of education and specialized training.

(3) To be the cultural centers for special lectures, programs, presentations of quality films, and other such activities. Whenever university extensions are established, there could be a direct tie into the local radio station.

• *The college with its extensions*. The college, of lower status than the university, but of high enough status to attract many students, would offer either a B.A. or a lower degree, concentrating on studies that include a broad liberal arts framework. The college would have as many provincial extensions as staff and funds would permit. First rank extensions would be in first class cities and second rank extensions in municipalities of ranks three to five. The Manila branch of the college might also attract first class city students. First class city extensions would likely attract students from the surrounding barrios as well as neighboring municipalities. Municipal extensions would draw students from surrounding barrios and neighboring lower ranked municipalities with their barrios. The college extensions would thus carry quality education closer to the barrio and encourage a higher level of education for the barrio student who now has a sound educational foundation of primary school and high school available to him by government decree.

• *The Manila school with its extensions*. The faculty and students of the Manila based school would be the finest available from non-Filipino and Filipino sources. Outsiders (who chose to work in the province or who had lower academic standing) and less highly qualified Filipinos, would teach in the extension schools. These extensions would be improved and upgraded by improving the quality of the education of the new faculty and by encouraging the practice of visiting lectureships from the Manila schools.

This system of a Manila-based school with extensions would provide a natural screening program for students. Further, every student would become an apprentice teacher being trained as a teacher for a full-orbed role within society.

Pastoral training

One type of special education which is of interest to many North Americans is pastoral training. This would be carried out primarily by pastors who draw apprentice pastors around them (see figure 13). Apprentices would live in dormitories at the church or in the community, would work with the pastor in his everyday ministry, and would take courses at one of the provincial extensions of Manila schools. These courses would be designed for a pastoral ministry or a teaching ministry. In this way

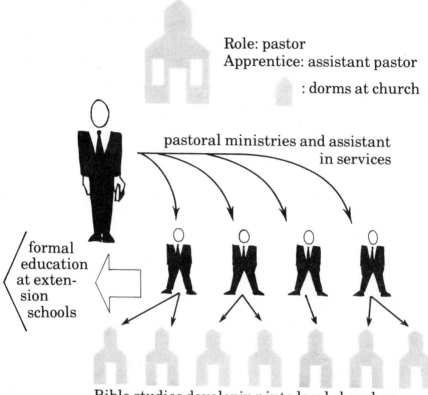

Role: pastor
Apprentice: assistant pastor

: dorms at church

pastoral ministries and assistant
in services

formal
education
at exten-
sion
schools

Bible studies developing into local churches

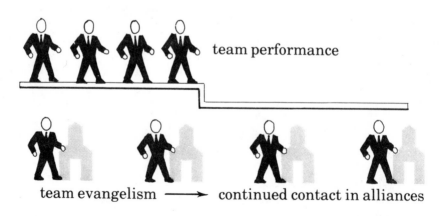

team performance

team evangelism ⟶ continued contact in alliances

Figure 13. **Pastoral Training Plan**

the pastoral training program would be a center for church development in the local area. The presence of educational institutions would mean the pastoral student could get a more formal education that would expand his horizons as well as improve his relationship with the people to whom he ministers. Every eligible pastoral student would spend only one year in Manila to complete his education and receive a diploma from a Manila school.

Pastors could be recruited from the United States, from among Christian scholars and educators in the Philippines, and from Filipino laymen wishing to enter the pastoral ministry. The apprentices would assist the master pastor in every aspect of the ministry as opportunity arises, would be responsible for barrio chapels, would carry out team evangelism and would sponsor special church programs. Uniformity of practice, doctrine, and training would be controlled through the educational institution. More promising students could thus be given as much formal education as possible without distracting them from their primary ministry. Pastors could, in effect, be trained in their local areas, using them where they are known, and letting the home folks share in their improved status through education.[3]

Program development consultant

Program extension would result in the development of a church, rural health care, or other institutional programs. The provincial worker (see figure 14) would become a program development consultant with a central office from which he and his staff could make contacts in the area. Each staff member of the development consultant office would work as an apprentice until he learned his role. Eventually, one or more apprentices could be assigned to him, and offices would be scattered throughout the geographic area. The staff would be responsible for identifying each alliance head within the community by conducting an ongoing survey throughout the first years of the developing program. Attention would be given to each contact to determine whether that contact is the real alliance leader or not. Staff responsibility would be to identify these leaders and to continue contact with as many as were willing. They would proceed by special assignment to establish interpersonal relationships with as many heads of alliances as is feasible. Records would be kept of all contacts and all developments within the relationship. Discussions within the staff would then center on activities that would aid in building a continuing relationship with these people.

The staff would be assigned to associate with different alliance heads on the basis of their relative status within the community. For example,

109

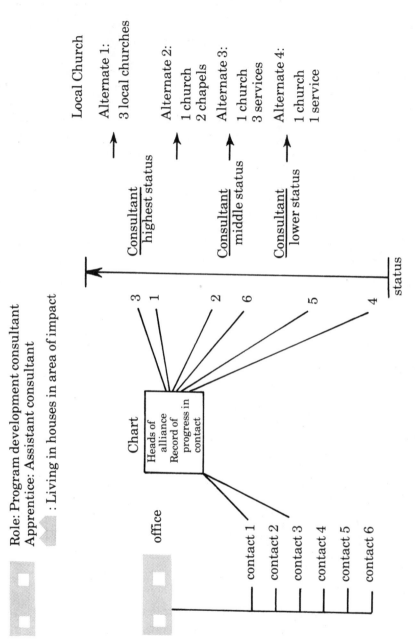

Figure 14. **Program Development Consultant**

someone working in Lipa City with the highest perceived status would be wise to join Rotary; middle status would join the Jaycees; and lower status would work with barrio groups.

A person of high status could work with people of lower status for a short period of time, but ideally the principle of status should be maintained for the good of the work and for establishing enduring trust relationships.

Student work in the provincial extensions of the college or university could also be used to make contacts and to establish enduring relationships with leaders. Each development consultant, according to his background and training, might be invited to lecture in the provincial schools.

In the early stages of the program, special attention should be given to personal contacts, and local groups established as there is need. Tagalog will not merge comfortably with Chinese; upper status people will not interact over a period of time with lower status people. The group development consultant should determine how many local groups are needed. It is possible that one group could serve each social strata with separate meetings for the different smaller groups. It would be wise for the leaders of each alliance within the group to decide which of the alliances will have the highest status, rather than forcing incompatible alliances together.

Another important responsibility for the development consultant would be to encourage the alignment of alliances under a personality figure. In time this would produce strength as well as increase outreach potential.

The development consultant would also be responsible to see that interpersonal relationships are maintained smoothly. The progress of teacher and apprentices should be under his continuing supervision.

The provincial worker often has his long range goal clearly in mind, and the short range goal expressed as, "Well, I have to do something." But this suggested program gives him not only a middle range to work towards but specific day-to-day responsibilities that will ultimately contribute to his short range and long range goals.

Notes and references

[1] For further discussion of this concept, see Walden F. Bello. "Brain Drain in the Philippines." *Modernization: Its Impact in the Philippines IV*. IPC Papers, No. 7. Ateneo de Manila University Press, Quezon City, 1969, 93–146.

[2] One serious problem faced in the Philippines is that a youth finds a girl from some other province and marries her during his Manila-based studies. If he is assigned to his own province, his wife is unhappy. If he is assigned to his wife's region, he knows no one and

111

takes years to get established. If he is assigned to yet a third region, both he and his wife are misplaced, and much time is needed to become trusted and to work into the mutual obligation pattern.

[3] For background reading on education in the Philippines, see:

Vitaliano Bernardino. *The Philippine Community School*. Phoneix Press, 1958.

Jaime Bulatao. "The Conflict of Values in Home and School." *The Guidance and Personnel Journal*. Manila, Vol. I, No. 1, November, 1965, 50–53.

———. "Personal Preferences of Filipino Students." *Philippine Sociological Review*. Vol. 11, No. 3–4, 1963, 168–178.

Arthur L. Carson. *Higher Education in the Philippines*. Bulletin No. 29, OE–14065. U.S. Department of Health, Education and Welfare, Office of Education, U.S. Government Printing Office, Washington, D.C., 1961.

John Carroll. "Education," in *Changing Patterns of Social Structure in the Philippines, 1896–1963*. Ateneo de Manila University Press, Quezon City, 1968, 45–53, 148–166.

Gelia Castillo. "Implications of Occupational Research on the Role of the Counselor in High School." *Philippine Sociological Review*. Vol. 13, No. 3, July, 1965, 149–150.

Vicente G. Sinco. *Education in Philippine Society*. University of the Philippines, Quezon City, 1959.

George Smith. "Education," in *Area Handbook on the Philippines*. Fred Eggan, et al., Supervisors. University of Chicago for Human Relations Area Files, 1956, Vol. II, 745–995.

Chapter 15

Orientation to Bicultural Living

Although English is spoken, language learning is imperative in the Philippines. Tagalog is both spoken and lived, and every person dealing in any way with Filipinos must be fluent in Tagalog or one of the other languages spoken there. A well-oriented person is characterized by being able to shift to Tagalog when the Filipino is ready. This shift may never happen with some, but if it does, and the North American is not ready to go along, the friendship will deteriorate rather than develop.

In the provincial areas especially, it appears that the use of English is decreasing, a development which must be taken into account. Parents who start instructing their children in English as soon as they begin to talk grow discouraged since the older children have limited opportunities to use it.

Every person who enters the Philippines to serve the Filipino needs a basic language and culture orientation. Information about the country and people can be acquired by extensive reading, but attitudes and adaptations of lifestyle require special help by someone already having gone through the acculturation process. The urgency for the orientation and its thoroughness may depend upon the role the newcomer expects to have in the Filipino society. Those in categories one to three below need more orientation than those in categories four and five.

(1) Teachers or workers in urban areas.

(2) Provincial workers.

(3) Secretaries and assistants in the offices of educational institutions.

(4) Workers who have only minimal contact with Filipinos, or who relate to them in only one way.

(5) People who deal only with English speakers in the country.

Techniques for the orienter

(1) Encourage an attitude that Tagalog is necessary for effective communication.

(2) Build initial lessons around useful conversation so that the student can go out and practice immediately (rote memory).

(3) Increase usefulness of conversation by developing simple substitution frames, using the same grammatical structures that occur in conversation.

(4) Use as little English as possible. When teaching new material, describe the situation in English, then use Tagalog within the situation.

(5) Give more drill for significant differences. Use a rule for less significant differences.

(6) Use extra drills for whatever is confusing to a North American.

(7) Put the most frequently used items in the first lessons.

(8) Make a series of sentences hang together whenever possible.

(9) Have student memorize characteristic folklore, especially in the early stages of language learning.

(10) Encourage use of tape loops, i.e. a loop of tape which takes thirty to sixty seconds for one round and is left on the machine to go around and around. This is an excellent exercise for repetition of material needing memorization.

(11) Concentrate the initial language learning program into a fairly intensive period, and then have workshops once or twice a year to work on specific language problems.

(12) Utilize as many kinds of cultural orientation situations as possible to discover cues to both verbal and nonverbal communication.

Practice situations for the student

There are two ways for the student to learn from his day-to-day contacts and experiences: (1) He should observe nonverbal cues in social activities in which he may participate, such as at a wedding, a baptism, a banquet, or other; and (2) he can learn from verbal experiences, either written or spoken in monologues, dialogue, discussion, demonstration,

114

simulation, and discovery/experience. Following are some suggested exercises which may be simulated by role play, or which he may experience in real life.

(1) Give a gift or loan something.

(2) Keep the Filipino from putting you on the spot.

(3) Help by action as well as by asking "What can I do to help?"

(4) Bargain in the store or marketplace.

(5) Take a circle route on a jeepney.

(6) Practice using euphemism instead of "no."

(7) Practice a different day schedule.

(8) Note the "presence," i.e. the sense that someone is watching you. This may be evidenced by a potential pickpocket at the airport, a girl chasing flies at the table, barrio people standing around while you eat, stares on the street, market awareness, children watching while waiting for a jeepney, people looking out from a house or store window as you pass by, children and maids going through the drawers in your room, a door being opened without your knocking, someone turning on lights as you move from room to room, or not being left alone in a room.

(9) Make an unannounced visit to a Filipino home.

(10) Practice tactile or touch behavior such as a woman putting her arm around another woman's arm or around her shoulders; a man holding another man's hand.

(11) Serve *merienda* to unexpected visitors.

(12) Cordially invite an unexpected visitor to a meal. Don't take the first answer as final, ask a second or third time.

(13) Leave some food on the serving plate.

(14) Don't serve/eat solid food after a beverage.

(15) Don't admire any "portable" item.

(16) Remember that meal time is not a talking time unless the host chooses to make it so.

(17) Don't "paw" over the children.

(18) Accept the fact that "Thank you" ends it; equals pay.

(19) Remember that the host and/or hostess do not have to partake of a meal.

(20) Taste each food offered.

(21) Practice "status talk" to the maid, to an important political figure, or to someone else. This can be done through directed role play where the leader of the program enlists the help of a member of the group. Each, within his role, proceeds to talk through an encounter of boss with maid, or individual with authority figure.

(22) Play the systems game *Strata*, available through Associates of Urbanus, Farmington, Michigan. This is a simulation that is designed to let one learn the unknown roles of a stratification system that he will meet in some form everywhere in the Philippines. This game can be played by twenty to forty people in an hour.

(23) Practice status introductions. Who is introduced to whom and how much is indicated about each person—more for members of the alliance, less for nonmembers; more for higher status people, less for lower status.

Notes and references

For additional materials on specific orientation to the Philippines and general preparation for bicultural living, see:

George M. Guthrie. "Cultural Preparation for the Philippines," edited by Robert B. Textor, *Cultural Frontiers of the Peace Corps*. The Massachusetts Institute of Technology Press, Massachusetts, 1966.

Frank Lynch and Mary Hollnsteiner. *Understanding the Philippines and America: A Study of Cultural Trends*. Institute of Philippines Culture Publications, Ateneo de Manila University Press, Quezon City, 1966.

Marvin K. Mayers. *Christianity Confronts Culture*. Zondervan, Grand Rapids, Michigan, 1974.

John R. Snarey. *AnthroPAULogist*. A course in crosscultural interpersonal relations. LEE: Leader Education Enterprises, Box 788, Wheaton, Illinois, 1974.

Appendix 1

A Survey of Philippine History

Every visitor in the Philippines needs to understand the social, economic, religious and political systems. Analysis of present conditions and participation in the culture is necessary for maximum communication; but a study of past events and people's responses to them deepens the understanding. The picture of the Philippines becomes more complete as one reviews its struggles, goals, and development.

Of the many people who reached the Philippines, the oldest were probably the negritos, a branch of the negroid stock that came around 25,000 years ago. Succeeding groups of inhabitants are difficult to distinguish. Some anthropologists identify the next arrivals as proto-Malay who penetrated the interior and supposedly introduced agriculture.

Then Malays arrived from Western Indonesia and Borneo around 300 to 200 B.C. spreading to the coastal regions of Visayas, Mindanao, Mindoro, and southern Luzon. They brought iron-age tools, a knowledge of smelting and forging iron, glassmaking, new techniques of weaving, and the system of rice cultivation by paddies with dykes.[1] They differed from the previous inhabitants in their way of living as regards use of boats, architecture, and dress.

During the next few hundred years the islands' trade grew with Indonesia. In the tenth century India established contact with Sulu and imported abaca, coconut, cottons, and aromatic woods.

Indonesian refugees, arriving in the thirteenth and fourteenth centuries, spread Islam in Sulu, Mindanao, and the northern areas. In the mid-fourteenth century the Philippines came under the domination of Java, stimulating trade. During the fifteenth century China attempted to control the islands, and appointed a governor for Luzon who exacted tribute. Thus in early times, the Philippines came partially under the influence of Asia, the Middle East, and the great Eastern cultures.

The diversified peoples of the Philippines developed a similarity in culture and lifestyle with the immediate and extended family as the basic unit of social organization. In pre-Spanish days polygamy was not widespread. It was practiced by the wealthy, usually Moslems. Divorce and remarriage could be obtained through: (1) failure to have children; (2) prolonged illness; or (3) an opportunity for a more advantageous marriage. Still, divorce was the exception. Parents negotiated their children's marriage to cement kinship alliances and property arrangements. The groom paid the father-in-law or worked for him, living at his home. The couple had opportunity for premarital relations, for the final ceremony might be postponed until the bride showed she could become a mother.[2]

The *barangay*, a unit of political organization, was a kinship group consisting of thirty to a hundred related families, with as many as two thousand people. The people were economically dependent on the leader who was the political authority for their locality.[3]

Moslems also had the concept of king or chief called the *datu*. Lynch says, "Pre-Spanish society consisted of chiefly class (*datus* and their families and the freemen) and non-chiefly class (freemen, bondsmen or tenants, and slaves). The two classes were linked by ties of political dependence."[4]

The people were primarily agricultural. The communal title to a property area was vested in the *barangay*. They raised rice and root crops supplemented with fish, swine, and fowl.

Except for Moslems, the preconquest religion of the Filipinos was a blend of monotheism and polytheism. They emphasized ancestor and nature worship, and had charms to protect them from illness.[5] Their concept of a supreme being was one who created the universe and ruled men, and who was surrounded by gods, goddesses, and spirits. Prayers and sacrifices were offered to placate the spirits, some of whom were intermediaries between the living and the dead. But they did not build temples and they never believed blood from human sacrifices nourished the gods.[6]

Spanish domination of the Philippines was the culmination of an eighth century expansionist movement, with two goals: military domination, and conversion to Christianity. In America and the Orient, the idea of suppressing paganism was supplemented by the Christian-humanist idea that the people must be given "superior" western culture with Christianity.

Spain's interest in the Philippines was apparent when she and Portugal signed the Treaty of Tordesillas in 1493. Prior to this, Pope

Alexander had established the Line of Demarcation dividing the world into two spheres of influence—Spanish and Portuguese. The Line was moved eight hundred miles west, giving Brazil to Portugal and the Philippines to Spain. By 1510 Spain had established maritime control of the Indian Ocean.

In 1519 Magellan sailed from Seville, searching for the western passage to the south seas and hoping for an opportunity to cash in on the profitable spice trade. As a result of his efforts to Christianize a few of the islands, they were called Islas Filipinas after Philip II in 1542. But the Spaniards did not establish control of the country until Legaspi conquered Cebu in 1565 and established a settlement and mission. Though Moslems were entrenched in the south, their control of the north and central areas was superficial.

The sudden intrusion of the Spanish military, church, and government was less damaging psychologically and physically for the Filipinos than for other victims of colonization because they were adaptable. They preserved their uniqueness by taking the outward forms of Spanish culture and adapting them to their own ends.[7]

The Philippine conquest was relatively bloodless. Philip was influenced by two Dominican friars who adopted Thomas Aquinas' idea that pagan peoples do not lose their social, political, and economic rights merely by coming in contact with Christians. The rights that all peoples enjoy by virtue of natural law must be considered by a Christian nation, seeking to work with those people.[8]

The three primary objectives in keeping the Philippines were: (1) to share in the spice trade, a Portuguese monopoly; (2) to have direct contact with China and Japan; and (3) to Christianize the native.[9]

The first years of Spanish occupation were spent recovering from economic disasters. There were rice shortages in the 1570's and 1580's. Later rice production was increased, though little was done to improve methods or technology. A part of the population who had been mobile shifting cultivators became permanent field farmers, making it easier to tax them, to Christianize them, and to secure the desired labor services.[10]

The Spaniards sought grants of land called *encomiendas* which carried the right to levy commodity tribute and labor from the peoples living there—a sort of feudal system. However, the *encomiendas* did not bring Spain great wealth, for the Filipinos adapted their native system of power to the Spanish plan. The heads of each community could acquire official titles to the land, thus legalizing the preconquest societal control of the dependent class. A great division existed between large landowners and poor tenant farmers; it was easier to remain in the tenant class than to accumulate enough wealth to buy out of it.

Spain profited primarily through the galleon trade from Manila to China and Mexico. Merchants traded Chinese silks in Acapulco for Mexican silver. Unfortunately, this benefited only a few merchants, not the island government.

Many Chinese emigrated to the Philippines. Their commercial skill was admired. Yet they were distrusted, feared, and even killed. For though the Philippines needed their skills, Filipinos resented the Chinese control of their wealth, business and property.

The Spanish tried to help the Filipinos establish local governments. But the people resented resettlement, preferring to live close to their rice fields. There was little inducement for them to move into the towns, although they came in periodically for church rituals. The priests began to use *visita* chapels in the outlying areas, and held services on a rotating basis. As it was, although most Filipinos came into some contact with Spanish culture, it was not sustained or prolonged enough to assimilate the people. The Tagalogs who lived in the area surrounding Manila, the seat of Spanish authority, were greatly affected by Spanish control and influence.

Spain's primary agents for holding the territory and assuring some allegiance were the missionary priests. The priests found that getting the people to accept Christianity was relatively easy, for they spread the belief that baptism not only wiped away the sins of the soul but also helped cure the body.[11]

The priests were not welcome in all areas. The mountain peoples and negritos strongly resisted them, as did the Moslems (Moros) in the south. While the conversion to Christianity was fairly rapid for most of the country, it was superficial. Their inner loyalty to old beliefs took the outward form of Christianity for social convenience.[12]

One barrier hindering communication was language. Though priests intended to bring their message in the local dialect, it was not often done; and their instruction in Spanish was completely inadequate. Nearly four hundred years after Spanish rule, it was estimated that no more than ten percent of the population knew Spanish.

A logical solution would have been to train Filipino priests, educate them thoroughly in the faith, and let them work among their own people. Pope Pius XII later said in his encyclical letter, ". . . let us call to your attention how important it is that you build up a native clergy. If you do not work with all your might to accomplish this, we maintain that your apostolate will not only be crippled, but it will prove to be an obstacle and an impediment for the establishment and organization of the Church in those countries."[13] The failure of the church in the Philippines to realize this was a tremendous mistake.

120

The main reasons why it was not done were: (1) the clergy's desire to preserve their power and privileges, and (2) their idea that the Filipinos were not fit, for their interest in the priesthood appeared to arise from status considerations rather than spiritual ones.

Archbishop Rufina tried in 1767 to implement the policy of a native clergy, but there was a lack of qualified Filipino priests and those in office performed poorly. This substantiated the fears of the religious hierarchy.

The Spanish conquest affected the family also by introducing the *compadrazgo* system which promoted stable interclass and intergroup relations.

Politically, the Filipinos adapted to the Spanish conquest. The magistrates were often affluent Filipinos who organized the population for the benefit of the colonial government. They played a creative role as intermediaries between the two cultures. Political offices in each community were monopolized by a small group of bosses known as *caciques*. Few people participated in government due to this control and also due to the people's limited education and knowledge of Spanish. However, the population did not accept the abuse of the Spanish church and state or the collaboration of their own upper class. Over one hundred revolts flared during the 333 years of Spanish rule; but still Spain would not initiate reforms.

During the nineteenth century unrest grew among the Spanish American colonies. Mexico achieved independence in 1821. About that time other Latin American countries also won their freedom.

Opening the Suez Canal brought foreign commercial interest to the Philippines. Increased prosperity made it possible for Filipinos to attend European universities where they came in contact with liberal ideas. These Filipinos, influenced by events in Europe and America, began to discuss publicly Spain's failure to carry out promises for reforms in government and religion. A widespread dislike for friars grew and anti-Spanish feeling climaxed at the mutiny at Cavite in 1872 when three priests were executed.

José Rizal, son of a middle class landowner, was trained in Europe as a doctor, linguist, and author. He wrote two significant novels titled *Noli Me Tangere* (Don't Touch Me)[14] and *El Filibusterismo* (The Practice of Filibustering) in which he warned Spaniards that violent consequences might follow if the reformers were not punished when reforms were not carried out.

The government chose harsh suppression as its policy, however, and violence broke out. On December 26, 1896 Rizal appeared before a military court, was declared guilty, and shot by a firing squad because his writings had influenced others to attack the Spanish government.

Along with her interest in Cuba, the United States began to look toward the Philippines. Expansion had reached the borders of the North American continent by the 1890's, and Americans were looking for new territories to create growth in the nation's economy and to provide outposts for the nation's defense. After a build-up of events, the U.S. declared war on Spain on April 25, 1898. The Spanish fleet was destroyed and the Americans took possession of Cavite, the peninsula in Manila Bay.[15]

Filipino revolutionaries at first supported the American believing that they were liberators. But tensions soon arose between the Filipinos, who were determined to govern themselves, and the Americans. On June 12, 1898, Aguinalde declared the independence of the Philippines which America and other nations ignored. Later when the Philippines Republic was proclaimed, the United States was in the awkward position of balancing her ideals against self-interest. America was supposed to believe in a government "whose just powers are derived from the consent of the governed." But what about their commercial investment? What about their base in Asia as a foothold toward China and Japan? What about their protection against Russia, Germany, or any country which would infringe on China's "Open Door" policy?

A strong voice urging the U.S. to retain the Philippines was the evangelical church. Church boards and conferences urged that the States insure freedom and an open door to the Philippines. The determination, goals, and ambitions of the Filipinos were pushed aside and ignored consistently. In the Treaty of Paris the U.S. took complete possession of the islands and paid Spain a twenty million dollar indemnity. In August, 1898, the Spaniards surrendered Manila, Filipinos were ordered to stay out of the city, and the American flag was raised. The direct conflict which broke out between American and Filipino troops stretched into many bloody battles during a three year period leaving 250,000 dead.

The U.S. was determined to preserve her concept of superiority over these "primitive" peoples, but the Filipinos did not want to be ruled by the Americans now that they were rid of the Spaniards. After gaining control, the Americans modified their stance and let the Filipinos take important positions in government. They agreed that the Philippines would eventually gain their independence. Yet they wanted to be sure that the Filipinos had trained, qualified leaders. The United States set up as its goals: (1) a free and independent republic; (2) a free primary school system; and (3) the extension of government health services.

One area in which the U.S. had success was education. The first comprehensive school law was passed in January, 1901, which set up a highly centralized system. Hundreds of teachers were brought from the United States. Because of the variety of languages, instruction was in English. Education became the largest item in the budget of local and central government. The Philippines was significantly affected by the increase of education which was made available to large segments of the population. A great desire for western methods and technology was created. It is also interesting to note that education affected the stratification system of the Philippines in that it contributed to social mobility. Many lower status people moved up in status.

The U.S. also had success in improving the health of the Filipinos. After starting health services, developing pure water supplies, and opening government medical schools, the death rate fell especially as infant mortality decreased. However, the improved standards of living combined with Filipino family values sent the size of the population soaring, and placed an increasing burden on the country's resources and economy.

The Philippine's struggle for independence continued immediately after American control was established. The *Nationalista Partido* dominated every national election until 1946. The Jones Act stated that Filipinos were to be given independence as soon as they demonstrated they could govern themselves. But because of the family and alliance structure of society, the pattern of mutual obligation and responsibility, and the tendency to center leadership in the hands of a few, the Filipinos did not completely adopt the American system of government. Personalities predominated, not ideology. Party allegiance could shift rapidly as people owed their loyalty to the leader not to the party.[16] By 1920 many government officials were related and government positions were being bought through political influence. This was not the American ideal so the U.S. policy suffered a reversal for a while. The Philippine government was criticized, viewed as unstable, and was said to be unfit for independence.

Then policies became more liberal; for though the Americans desired to guide the Filipinos to political independence, their economic policies were not oriented toward self-sufficiency. While promoting Philippine self-reliance on one hand, American policy was encouraging dependence on the other. The economic dependence created mixed feelings. Nationalists wanted independence, but realistically, they knew they could not survive economically if the U.S. left completely.

The outbreak of World War II delayed the Philippines drive for independence. It is significant that a loyalty was shown by the Filipinos to the United States at this time. The Japanese tried to gain U.S. support but were unsuccessful. In spite of inequities of American rule, perhaps a reciprocal relationship had been built up between the two countries.

The postwar problems were tremendous—food shortages, inflation, blackmarket created by American surplus, and government corruption. In spite of this, however, the Philippines finally gained their independence in July, 1946. Manuel Roxas y Acuña became the first president. The country needed aid from the U.S., which gave billions of dollars but demanded parity rights giving U.S. business equal opportunities with Filipinos.

Then the problem with the Huks (a movement of dissatisfied farmers and workers which formed during the war) became more serious and Roxas' successor, Quirino, attempted to deal with them. It wasn't until Ramon Magsaysay was appointed Secretary of Defense that the government made any headway. He helped restore the Filipinos' confidence in their government. He ran for president in 1954, was elected and served with great popularity. He died in a plane crash in 1957.

In the next few years new political parties were formed and different groups fought for control. In 1961 Diosdado Macapagal was elected. He faced a national debt, an empty treasury, wide tax evasion, and rising unemployment. He pushed an ambitious agricultural reform law through Congress that abolished sharecropping tenancy, creating leasehold farmers who eventually held family-size farms, and provided technical aid and credit to new farm owners. However, rapid population growth helped defeat his programs. Ferdinand Marcos was elected in 1965 and in 1969. He, too, faced severe economic problems, problems of civil unrest, and organized crime in the Manila area.

Notes and references

[1] Raymond Nelson. *The Philippines*. New York, Walker and Company, 1968, 22.

[2] John L. Phelan. *The Hispanization of the Philippines*. Madison, Wisconsin, University of Wisconsin Press, 1959, 19.

[3] Nelson. 118.

[4] Frank Lynch. "Trends Report of Studies in Social Stratification and Social Mobility in the Philippines." *East Asian Cultural Studies*, 4, March 1965, 164–166.

[5] Nelson. 22.

[6] ———. 24.

[7] Fredrick L. Wernstedt and Joseph E. Spencer. *The Philippine Island World, A Physical, Cultural, and Regional Geography*. Berkeley, California, University of California Press, 1967, 120.

[8] Phelan. 9.

[9] ———. 7.

[10] Wernstedt. 26.

[11] Gerald H. Anderson, ed. *Studies in Philippine Church History*. Ithaca, New York, Cornell University Press, 1969, 37.

[12] Onofre Corpuz. *The Philippines*. Englewood Cliffs, New Jersey, Prentice-Hall, 1965, 35.

[13] Encyclical letter "Maximum illud." November 30, 1919, *Acta Apostolicae Sedis*, XI (1919), 444–45 (from Anderson, 65).

[14] *Noli Me Tangere* has been translated into English. See *The Lost Eden*, trans. by Leon ma Guerra, New York, Greenwood Press, 1968.

[15] For a full account of the events surrounding the U.S. acquisition of the Philippines, see *Little Brown Brothers* by Leon Wolff, Garden City, New York, Doubleday, 1961. This history is especially recommended for North American missionaries to the Philippines.

[16] Nelson. 131.

Appendix 2

History of Lipa City

The primary research for this volume was done while living in Lipa City, a typical city of the Philippines. During its early history, which dates back to the sixteenth century, Lipa occupied four other sites before finally becoming established at its present location. The eruptions of the Taal volcano were responsible for three of these moves.

Lipa was first known as Tagbakin and located in the southeastern regions of Bombon Lake. At that time it was a settlement of thousands of people with well-built homes. Agriculture and commerce flourished. Salcedo, the brave grandson of Legaspi had been unbeaten in his many exploits, but when he tried to subdue the Lake Bombon region in 1574, he was repulsed by a strong army of 16,000 men. Later, the intrepid Marshal Gabriel de Rivera conquered the lake region. As a reward for this conquest he received authorization from Spain to permanently control the area, a control that was to be passed on to his heirs.

A group of Augustinian missionaries led by Hernando de Cabrera reached the settlement in 1605 and Tagbakin became both a town and a mission and was named San Sebastian after its patron saint. This patron saint, according to tradition was responsible for the first move. One day the image of the patron saint disappeared from the church. It was finally found some distance from the lake under a lipa tree in the mountainous region now known as Lumang Lipa. The saint must have wanted to live in that area where the image was found, so the people reasoned, and the town was moved there. At the same time its name was changed from San Sebastian to Lipa.

Because of the eruptions of the Taal Volcano, Lipa later moved eastward into a mountainous region. But there was no room for expansion at that location because of the mountains and the next move was to the more level site of Balete. Again the Taal Volcano erupted covering Lipa in Balete with lava and ashes in 1756 and Lipa moved this time to far distant highlands.

In 1774 the most destructive eruption of Tall occurred destroying the towns of Taal, Talisay, Tanaun, and Lipa. Fearing future eruptions, the people of all of these towns moved from the area, and Lipa went to the highland site that it still occupies.

From the arrival of the Augustinians until 1702, the settlement was not a municipality but a town and missionary site for the propagation of Catholicism. In 1702 it became a municipality. In 1887, Queen Cristina of Spain honored it with the title of Villa de Lipa. It wasn't until August of 1948 that Lipa became an established city under the mayorship of Esteban Mayo.

Various interesting incidents happened through the years. In 1757, Nicolas Bravo, who was governor at the time, gave orders for the people to gather stones from the seashore and bricks from the ruins of past townsites and bring them to the highlands for the construction of the first church and tower.

In 1763, British troops came in pursuit of the Spanish ship, Galleon Filipino, laden with a vast amount of wealth from Spain. The Spaniards were attempting to hide the wealth and prevent it from being taken by the British. It was a successful maneuver because the British never found the ship and its treasure.

Tobacco was an important crop of the region and in 1782 the first tobacco monopoly was introduced in Lipa under the leadership of Pascual Gutierrez. The people felt the hardship of the restrictions on their right to plant, to sell, or even to smoke the tobacco they themselves produced.

The first scaffold for the execution of outlaws was erected in 1787 in front of the school called Pia. This was under the governorship of Bernabe Laguerta. And in 1796, all the young men of Lipa were conscripted into the Spanish army. Baltazar de Africa was mayor at the time.

One of the most colorful governors of Lipa's early existence was Pablo Maralit who was known for his many miraculous deeds.

In 1802 a system of fixing boundaries was introduced under the leadership of Filipe Teodoro. Three years later the people faced starvation because of a severe famine.

The cultivation of coffee began in 1808 when Governor Galo de los Tayes commanded the people to plant coffee. Thus began the "Coffee Days" which brought wealth, splendor, and fame to Lipa. Between the years of 1843 and 1890 Lipa was one of the coffee producing centers of the world and the wealth of both Europe and America flowed into the area. It was during these golden years that Queen Cristina honored it with the title of Villa de Lipa.

In the barrios (outlying villages) of Lipa (see figure 15) and on the surrounding mountains, coffee plantations flourished. During coffee harvest season, the main streets of the city were filled with hundreds of carts pulled by cows and carabaos carrying coffee beans to be dried and stored in the huge warehouses. There were many stores and bazaars owned largely by Chinese, Indian, and Jews, and filled with commodities imported from Europe, America, and Asia.

Later the coffee industry met with disaster. In 1888 the last colorful procession celebrating the coffee harvest moved through the streets of Lipa. The next year the coffee trees began to die, killed by a certain kind of fungus that sapped the juice of the trees.

Even during the coffee days there were disasters for Lipa. The people believed that a comet with a long tail which streaked across the sky in 1841 foretold disasters. Shortly after, a revolt in the nearby town of Tayabas caused the death of many people including women, children, and the aged. In 1852 there were so many severe earthquakes that the Christmas midnight mass was not held. In 1858, a Spaniard by the name of Gregorio Aguilera arrived from Spain to collect extra tribute from those who did not like to labor in the public works.

Ten years later still another disaster struck Lipa. A fire burned the southeastern portion of the city, and the following year fire burned the entire city including the coffee trees in nearby areas.

However, because of the coffee industry, the people were prosperous and they built new and bigger houses with galvanized iron imported from Europe and the best timber from the mountains. Courtyards, art, architecture, carvings, statues, and decorations were patterned after the mansions and castles of the barons and the wealthy of Europe.

Epidemics also troubled the city. Asiatic cholera swept the entire southern Luzon regions in 1882 and Lipa was one of the cities affected. Later a beri-beri epidemic hit the city, to be followed by smallpox in 1889.

Lipa was especially hard hit by destruction during World War II. The people were taken by surprise by an invasion of the Japanese—something they did not anticipate would happen so quickly. Most of them evacuated the city proper and fled to remote barrios. Only a few remained in the city to witness the destruction. The Cathedral and the Episcopal Palace were the pride of Lipa but they were destroyed along with many beautiful homes. A few ruins of the homes destroyed remain including the foundations of the famous house of Don Fidel A. Reyes and portions of

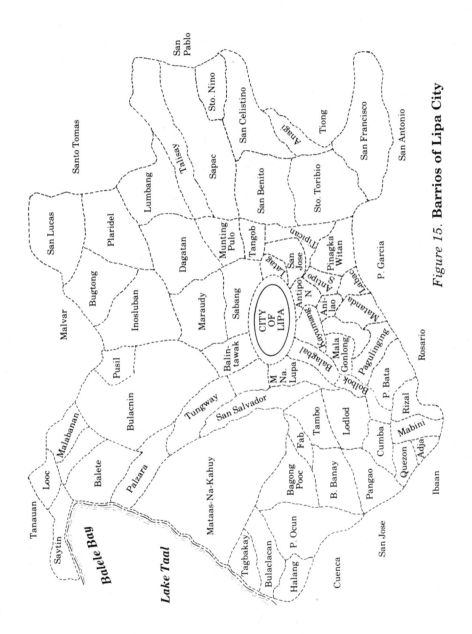

Figure 15. **Barrios of Lipa City**

the Bartolome Katigbak residence, especially the classic columns which were a part of the beautiful architecture.

Ruins still exist that date back into the beginnings of Lipa history for they are found on all of the previous sites of the city. After the eruption of the Taal Volcano in 1911, the wooden frame of an old adobe church together with religious paraphernalia was found floating on the lake shore near Tagbakin. This church is believed to be the first one built in Tagbakin early in the seventeenth century and later buried under the water. The stone foundation of the church erected in Lumang Lipa and the walls of the church ruins in Balete are still visible.

During the Japanese occupation a private home near the former municipal building was the headquarters for the military rule. Innocent Filipinos, suspected of being guerrillas or spies were imprisoned in this house and many more suffered cruelties at the hands of the Japanese. There was also a garrison where many, accused of various crimes, were brutally punished, beaten or given the water cure.

During the early part of the occupation, Mayor Pablo Torres was murdered somewhere between the barrios of Antipolo and Anilao. The motive was believed to be political, and the killers were soon caught and shot by Japanese authorities.

In the latter part of the Japanese occupation the officers made a public announcement that all male citizens should report at the city proper and they would be given a pass allowing them to go from one place to another without Japanese harrassment. The Filipinos, believing the announcement, went immediately to ask for the pass. They never returned.

Among the few houses left intact during the Japanese occupation are two interesting structures: those of Mr. Teofilo Maralit and Mrs. Josefa Librea Bautista. The first, about 200 years old, is the oldest building in the city. It has undergone repairs several times but still retains its high old-fashioned roof. The second house mentioned is typical of the coffee-boom mansions.

At the present time there are many modern homes and buildings in Lipa. Two of the most famous are the Carmel Chapel and the rebuilt Cathedral. The Carmel Chapel is considered the most modern and beautiful in the Philippines. It is of Romanesque architecture with stained glass windows and has a dome considered to be the highest in the Philippines. Other important and attractive landmarks are the Redemptorist church and monastery, the St. Paul Convent, the Bishops Palace and the Junior Seminary of Saint Francis of Salas.

Through the many generations of Lipa's history, the city has felt the devastations of volcanic eruptions, earthquakes, disastrous fires, famine, epidemics, and ravages of war. It has relocated, rebuilt, and known years of peace, prosperity and fame. The disasters and achievements of the past have blended together to make Lipa what it is today, a beautiful, thriving modern city of the Philippines.

Glossary

affinal	marriage relationship
amor propio	self love
barong Tagalog	special Filipino shirt, comparable to tuxedo
compadrazgo	system of godparenthood
compadre	godparent, i.e. sponsor of child at birth
cursillo	a directed learning retreat lasting a few days or weeks
higanti	vengeance
hiya	embarrassment or shame
kakulangan	recognized need
hasukat	one on same level as lender of money
kinakapatid	children of godparents
kulasisi	a steady girlfriend
lechon	a roast pig
malakas	has good connections, would be successful in getting money loan
mamamanhikan	from root *panhik* meaning "to go up the stairs"
merienda	snack time, coffee break

nagatatanim	literally means "planting;" an idiomatic expression showing idea that person cannot forget or forgive a hurt
ngali	customs, manners or habits
ninas kogon	something started enthusiastically but then dropped when enthusiasm waned
pahingi	a person in need goes to someone and attempts to collect on *utang na loob*
pakikisama	smooth, congenial companionship
pakinsapan	mediator talks victim into agreeing with request
pasalobong	gift brought back from a trip
polo barong	sport version of *barong Tagalog*, equivalent of western type sports jacket
prologamen	leading gradually to request
sagana	recognized surplus to fulfill specific recognized need
SIR	smooth interpersonal relations
umaakyat ng ligair	the Filipino dating period with marriage definitely in mind; translated it means "going up to court someone," or "up a staircase"
utang na loob	debt of primary obligation

Bibliography

READING

(Selected printed materials including books, reports, and articles.)

Abueva, Jose V. *Focus on the Barrio.* Institute of Public Administration, University of the Philippines, Manila, 1959.

Achutegui, Pedro S. and Miguel A. Bernard. *Religious Revolution in the Philippines.* Vol. 1, Ateneo de Manila, 1961.

————. *Religious Revolution in the Philippines.* Vol. 2, Ateneo de Manila, 1966.

Afable, Lourdes. "The Muslims as an Ethnic Minority in the Philippines." *Philippine Sociological Review.* Vol. 8, No. 1–2, January-April, 1960, 16–33.

Amyot, Jacques. *The Chinese Community of Manila: A Study of Adaptation of Chinese Familism to the Philippines Environment.* Philippine Studies Program, Department of Anthropology, University of Chicago, Chicago, Illinois, 1960.

————. "The Problem of Values in Social Anthropology." *Philippine Sociological Review.* Vol. 7, 1959, 1–6.

Anderson, Gerald. *Studies in Philippine Church History.* Cornell University Press, Ithaca, New York, 1969, 421 pp. (An ecumenical collection of essays presenting the basic history of the Christian Church in the Philippines from the time of the Spanish conquest to the present.)

———— and Peter G. Gowing. "Four Centuries of Christianity in the Philippines: An Interpretation." *Encounter.* Vol. 25, No. 3, Summer, 1964, 352–367.

Ando, Hirofumi. "The Iglesia ni Cristo in the 1965 Philippines." Center for South and Southeast Asian Studies Democratic Development Seminar Working Paper No. 3, August 26, 1966.

———. "Study of Iglesia ni Cristo: A Politico-Religious Sect in the Philippines." *Pacific Affairs*. Vol. 42, Fall, 1969, 334–345.

———. "A Study of the Linguistic Factor in the Philippine Elections." Center for South and Southeast Asian Studies Democratic Development Seminar Working Paper No. 8, December, 1966.

Angeles, Noli de los. "Marriage and Fertility Patterns in the Philippines." *Philippine Sociological Review*. Vol. 13, No. 4, October, 1965, 232–248.

Araneta, Francisco. "The Problem of Cultural Diversity." *Philippine Studies*. Vol. 12, No. 2, April, 1964, 232–243.

Arens, Richard. "Social Scientists Point the Way to Religious Acculturation and Accommodation." *Philippine Sociological Review*. Vol. 6, No. 1, January, 1958, 14–18.

Averech, Harvey, et al. *Matrix of Policy in the Philippines*. Rand Corporation Research Study, Princeton University Press, 1971.

Bare, Garland and William Reyburn. "Motives in Missionary Identification." *Practical Anthropology*. Vol. 10, 1963, 89–90.

Barnett, Milton L. "Hiya, Shame and Guilt: Preliminary Consideration of the Concepts vs. Analytical Tools for Consideration of Philippine Social Science." *Philippine Sociological Review*. Vol. 14, 1966, 276–291.

Barrows, David P. *A History of the Philippines*. American Book Company, New York, 1926, 406 pp.

Barton, Roy F. *Autobiographies of Three Pagans in the Philippines*. University Books, New Hyde Park, New York, 1963, 267 pp. (These three autobiographies, originally published under the title *Philippine Pagans: The Autobiographies of Three Ifugaos*, were originally recorded in Ifugao and then translated into English. The study presents insights into Ifugao marriage and courtship patterns.)

———. *The Half-Way Sun*. Brewer and Warren, New York, 1930, 316 pp. (An excellent semi-popular account of Ifugao religion.)

———. *Ifugao Economics*. University of California Publications in American Archaeology and Ethnology. Vol. 15, No. 5, 1922, 385–446.

———. *Ifugao Law*. University of California Press, Berkeley, 1969, 120 pp. (Barton's first major work, originally published in 1919, is a classic in Philippine ethnology. Although not always technically accurate, it is a pioneer study based on firsthand field research.)

———. *The Kalingas*. With an introduction by E. Adamson Hoebel. University of Chicago Press, 1949, 275 pp. (A comparative study of the Kalinga's social institutions and custom law.)

_____. *The Mythology of the Ifugaos*. Memoirs of the American Folklore Society, Vol. 46, American Folklore Society, Philadelphia, 1955.

_____. *The Religion of the Ifugaos*. Memoir No. 65, American Anthropological Association, Menasha, Wisconsin, 1946, 219 pp. (A comparative survey study of Ifugao religion. Again, he may not always be technically accurate but this is still a fine study based on firsthand field knowledge.)

Batacan, Delfin Fl. *Looking at Ourselves*. Philaw Publishing, Manila, 1956.(A self study of Filipino "peculiar" social traits.)

Bateson, Mary Catharine. "Insight in a Bicultural Context." *Philippine Studies*. Vol. 16, 1968, 605–621.

Beal, Alan R. *Culture in Process*. Holt, Rinehart and Winston, New York, 1967, 284 pp. (Unique in its emphasis on the inductive approach, this general introduction to cultural anthropology presents illustrative data first and generalizations second.)

Bellah, Robert N., ed. *Religion and Progress in Modern Asia*. Free Press, New York, 1965, 246 pp.

Bello, Walden F. "Brain Drain in the Philippines," in *Modernization: Its Impact on the Philippines IV*. IPC Papers, No. 7. Ateneo de Manila University Press, Quezon City, 1969, 93–146. (Discusses the emigration of the most talented and highly skilled Filipinos to the United States.)

_____ and Alfonso de Guzman II, eds. *Modernization: Its Impact in the Philippines III*. IPC Papers, No. 6. Ateneo de Manila University Press, Quezon City, 1968, 153 pp. (The phenomenon of modernization is subjected to further interdisciplinary study. Filipino interpersonal behavior patterns, a squatter community, autonomy, group judgments, and the diet of a Philippine rural community are discussed.)

_____ and _____, eds. *Modernization: Its Impact in the Philippines IV*. IPC Papers, No. 7. Ateneo University Press, Quezon City, 1969, 187 pp. (Discussion of urbanization of Manila, the brain drain, the *Cursillo*, a comparative analysis of communication networks, autonomy and dependency, infant and maternal nutrition, and four Tagalog communities, and the use of the accent in the Bilko language.)

_____ and Maria C. Roldan, eds. *Modernization: Its Impact in the Philippines*. IPC Papers, No. 4. Ateneo de Manila University Press, Quezon City, 1967, 133.

Benitez, Conrado. *History of the Philippines*. Revised edition. Ginn and Company, Boston, 1954, 522 pp. (A history textbook used in Filipino schools.)

Bernardino, Vitaliano. *The Philippine Community School*. Phoenix Press,

1958, 318 pp. (Discusses one of the movements in the Philippine school system.)

Berzina, M. Ya. and S.I. Bruk, eds. *Population of Indonesia, Malaya, and the Philippines*. Scholarly Book Translation Series, C.C.M. Information Corporation, N.Y., 1970.

Beyer, H. Otley. "Historical Introduction," in *Chinese Elements in the Tagalog Language*, by E.A. Manuel. Filipiniana Publications, Manila, 1948, 9–25.

————. "The Philippines Before Magellan." *Asia*. Vol. 21, 1921, 861–892, 924–970.

———— and Jaime C. de Veyra. *Philippine Saga: A Pictorial History of the Archipelago Since Time Began*. Capitol Publishing House, Inc., Manila, 1952, 152 pp.

Bonifacio, Manuel Flores. "Small Group Process and Social Change." *Philippine Sociological Review*. Vol. 9, No. 1–2, January-April, 1961, 20–29.

Braganza, Vicente. *The Encounter*. Catholic Trade School, San Carlos Publications, Manila, 1965, 235 pp. (An account of the "Christianization" of the Philippines.)

Bruton, William P. "New Movement in the Catholic Church: A study of the *Cursillo*," in *Modernization: Its Impact in the Philippines IV*. IPC Papers, No. 7. Ateneo de Manila University Press, Quezon City, 1969, 1–23. (A discussion of the *Cursillo* or "Little Course in Christianity" movement in the Philippines with a focus on the question, "Does the *Cursillo* really work?")

Buenaventura, Amparo S. "Some Problems Related to Filipino Multilingualism." *Philippine Sociological Review*. Vol. 11, No. 1–2, January-April, 1963, 142–147.

Bulatao, Jaime. "Changing Social Values." *Philippine Studies*. Vol. 10, No. 2, April 1962, 206–14.

————. "The Conflict of Values in Home and School." *The Guidance and Personnel Journal*. Manila, Vol. 1, No. 1, November, 1965, 50–53.

————. "Family Discipline for Democratic Living." *Sunday Times Magazine*. Vol. 18, No. 34, March 31, 1963, 20–22.

————. "Hiya." *Philippine Studies*. Vol. 12, No. 3, July, 1964, 424–38.

————. "The 'Hiya' System in Filipino Culture," in *Structure and Value Orientation*. Edited by F. Landa Jocano. Filipino Cultural Heritage Lecture Series, No. 2, Gem Publications, Philippine Women's University, Manila, 1966.

————. "The Manileño's Mainsprings," in *Four Readings on Philippine Values*. Third edition, revised and enlarged. Frank Lynch and Alfonso de Guzman II, eds. IPC Papers, No. 2, Ateneo de Manila University

Press, Quezon City, 1970, 89–114. (A study of Manila Filipino's values—the mainsprings of their life and actions—through the use of the TAT technique.)

———. "Personal Preferences of Filipino Students." *Philippine Sociological Review*. Vol. 11, No. 3–4, 1963, 168–78.

———. "The Society Page Its Value System." *Philippine Sociological Review*. Vol. 12, 1964, 139–50.

———. "Split-Level Christianity," in *Split-Level Christianity (and) Christian Renewal of Philippine Values*. Ateneo de Manila University Press, Quezon City, 1966. (Deals with the co-existence within the same Filipino of two or more cognitive and behavior or value systems which are inconsistent with each other.)

———. "Unfolding the Mystery: A Social-Psychological View of the Philippine Church." *Home Life*. St. Paul Publications, Manila, April, 1965, 41–47.

Carroll, John. *Changing Patterns of Social Structure in the Philippines, 1896–1963*. Ateneo de Manila University Press, Quezon City, 1968, 236 pp. (A comparative sociological analysis of the structure of Philippine society at two points in time to examine the nature of change and identify the groups that have been significant carriers of change.)

———. "The Filipino Dilemma." *Solidarity*. Vol. 3, No. 11, November, 1968.

Carson, Arthur L. *Higher Education in the Philippines*. Bulletin No. 29, OE–14065. U.S. Department of Health, Education and Welfare; Office of Education, U.S. Government Printing Office, Washington, D.C., 1961, 251 pp. (An historical survey of private and public education including a directory of colleges and universities.)

Casper, Leonard. *New Writing from the Philippines: a critique and anthology*. Syracuse University Press, Syracuse, New York, 1966, 411 pp. (A collection of some modern Filipino writings in English including plays, poems, and short stories.)

Castillo, Gelia. "Implications of Occupational Research on the Role of the Counselor in High School." *Philippine Sociological Review*. Vol. 13, No. 3, July 1965, 149–50.

———. "Occupational Sex Roles as Perceived by Filipino Adolescents." *Philippine Sociological Review*. Vol. 9, No. 1–2, January-April, 1961, 2–11.

———. "Some Insights on the Human Factor in Overcoming Barriers to Adequate Food Supply." *Philippine Journal of Nutrition*. No. 17, 1964, 134–147.

Christie, E.B. *The Subanun of Sindangan Bay*. Bureau of Science, Division of Ethnology Publications, Manila, No. 6, 1909.

Claver, Francisco. *Dinawat Ogil: High Datu of Namnam.* Provisional title, forthcoming IPC Publication. Ateneo de Manila University Press, Quezon City. (The author, a missionary, describes life in a datu-controlled area.)

Cole, F.C. "The Tinguian," in *Anthropological Series.* Vol. 14, No. 2, Publication 209, Field Museum of Natural History, Chicago, 1922, 231–493.

―――. "Traditions of the Tinguian," in *Anthropological Series.* Vol. 14, No. 1, Publication 180, Field Museum of Natural History, Chicago, 1915, 1–226.

Coller, Richard, et al. "A Sample of Courtship and Marriage Attitudes Held by U.P. Students." *Philippine Sociological Review.* Vol. 2, No. 3, October, 1954, 31–45.

―――. *Social Effects of Donated Radios on Barrio Life.* Study Series No. 14. Community Development Research Council, University of the Philippines, Quezon City, 1961, 94 pp.

Concepcion, Mercedes B. "Population Crisis: Fact or Fancy?" *Unitas.* Vol. 39, September, 1966, 338–39.

Conklin, Harold C. "Getting to Know a Hanunoo Girl," in Philip Bock, ed., *Culture Shock.* Alfred A. Knopf, N.Y., 1970, 230–245.

―――. "Hanunoo Color Categories," in Dell Hymes, *Language in Culture and Society.* Harper and Row, Publishers, New York, 1964, 189–192.

Constantino, Ernesto. *Ilokano Dictionary.* PALI Language Texts Series, Howard McKaughan, ed. University of Hawaii Press, 1971.

Constantino, Josefina D. "The Filipino Mental Make-up and Science." *Philippine Sociological Review.* Vol. 14, No. 2, January, 1966, 18–28.

Cordero, Felicidad V. and Isabel S. Panopio. *General Sociology: Focus on the Philippines.* College Professors Publishing Corporation, Manila, 1968, 465 pp. (An introductory textbook for college students with an emphasis on Philippine society and culture.)

Corpuz, Onofre D. *The Philippines.* Modern Nations in Historical Perspective series, Prentice-Hall, Englewood Cliffs, New Jersey, 1965, 149 pp. (An interpretation of Filipino history by a Filipino scholar with a discussion of such concepts as Christianization and the role of Christianity as an agent of change.)

Costa, Horacio de la. "The Concept of Progress and Traditional Values in a Christian Society." *Religion and Progress in Modern Asia.* Edited by Robert N. Bellah. Free Press, New York, 1965, 15–29.

―――. *The Jesuits in the Philippines, 1581–1768.* Harvard University Press, Cambridge, Mass., 1961, 702 pp.

―――. *Readings in Philippine History.* Bookmark, Manila, 1965, 351 pp. (Selected historical texts with a commentary.)

Cressy, Earl H. *Strengthening the Urban Church: Developing More and Stronger Urban Churches.* United Church of Christ in the Philippines, Manila, 1955.

Cretien, Douglas. "A Classification of Twenty-One Philippine Languages." *The Philippine Journal of Science.* Vol. 91, No. 4, December, 1962. (A linguistic study of Philippine languages.)

Cullum, Leo. A. "The University and the Development of Ideals and Moral Values." *Philippine Studies.* Vol. 3, September, 1957, 299–310.

Cutshall, Alden. *The Philippines: Nation of Islands.* D. Van Nostrand Company, Inc., New York, 1964, 134 pp. (The author, Professor of Geography at the University of Illinois, emphasizes the physical-cultural-political relationships and traces the influence of geography upon Philippine society.)

Cuyugan, Ruben Santos. "Socio-Cultural Change and the Filipino Family." *Science Review.* Vol. 2, No. 3, March, 1961, 203–205.

Davenport, William. "Nonunilinear Descent and Descent Groups." *American Anthropolgist.* Vol. 61, 1959, 557–72.

Davis, Frederick B. *Philippine Language Teaching Experiments.* Philippine Center for Language Study Monographs, No. 5, Oceana, 1968.

Deats, Richard L. *Nationalism and Christianity in the Philippines.* Southern Methodist University Press, Dallas, Texas, 1968, 207.

———. *The Story of Methodism in the Philippines.* Union Theological Seminary, National Council of Churches in the Philippines, Manila, 1964, 129 pp.

De Raedt, Jules. "Religious Representations in Northern Luzon." *Saint Louis Quarterly.* Baguio City, Vol. 2, No. 3, 1964, 245–348. (A comparative study of the Mountain Province peoples.)

De Roos, Robert and Ted Spiegel. "The Philippines." *National Geographic,* Vol. 130, No. 5, September, 1966, 301–351.

De Young, John. "Communication Channels and Functional Literacy in the Philippine Barrio." *Journal of Asian Studies.* Vol. 22, No. 1, November, 1962, 67–77.

Dobby, Ernest Henry G. *Southeast Asia.* John Wiley and Sons, Inc., New York, 1951, 415 pp. (Contains a discussion on the Philippine Islands.)

Doherty, John F. "The Image of the Priest: A Study in Stereotyping." *Philippine Sociological Review.* Vol. 12, No. 1–2, January-April, 1964, 70–76.

———. "Sociology and Religion: Religious Maturity." *Philippine Studies.* Vol. 12, No. 4, October, 1964, 681–98.

Dorn, Louis. "Philippine Language Trends." *Practical Anthropology,* Vol. 14, July-August, 1967, 174–185.

Douglas, Donald E. "On Sharing the Wealth Philippine Style." *Practical Anthropology*, Vol. 19, September-October, 1972, 207–213.

Dozier, Edward P. *The Kalinga of Northern Luzon, Philippines*. Holt, Rinehart and Winston, New York, 1967, 102 pp. (A case study in cultural anthropology based on Dozier's field work among the Kalinga people living in the Mountain Province of northern Luzon. Social organization, kinship, life cycle, religion, war, headhunting, and the peace pact institution are discussed.)

———. *Mountain Arbiters*. University of Arizona Press, Tucson, 1966, 299 pp. (A description of the changing life of the Northern Kalinga.)

Dunignan, Peter. "Early Jesuit Missionaries: A Suggestion for Further Study." *American Anthropologist*. Vol. 60, 1958, 725–32.

Eggan, Fred. "Cultural Drift and Social Change." *Current Anthropology*. Vol. 4, 1963, 347–356.

———. "Kinship; Introduction." *International Encyclopedia of the Social Sciences*. Vol. 8, 1968, 390–401. (Contains a comprehensive bibliography on the anthropological analysis of kinship.)

———. "Philippine Social Structure." *Six Perspectives on the Philippines*. Edited by George Guthrie. Bookmark, Manila, 1968.

———. "The Sagada Igorots of Northern Luzon," in *Social Structure in Southeast Asia*. Edited by G.P. Murdock. Viking Fund Publications in Anthropology, No. 29, Quadrangle Books, Chicago, 1960.

———. "Some Aspects of Culture Change in the Northern Philippines." *American Anthropologist*. Vol. 43, No. 1, January, 1941, 11–18.

———, Evett Hester, and Norton Ginsburg, supervisors. *Area Handbook on the Philippines*. University of Chicago for Human Relations Area Files. Subcontractor's monographs HRAF–16, Chicago–5, 1956, 4 volumes, 1832 pp. (These four volumes are very comprehensive in quantity yet somewhat uneven in quality. On the whole, an excellent systematic study.)

——— and Alfredo Pacyaya. "The Sapilada Religion: Reformation and Accommodation Among the Igorots of Northern Luzon." *Southwest Journal of Anthropology*. Vol. 18, 1962, 95–113.

——— and William H. Scott. "Ritual Life of the Igorots of Sagada: Courtship and Marriage." *Ehtnology*. Vol. 4, 1965, 77–111.

——— and ———. "Ritual Life of the Igorots of Sagada: From Birth to Adolescence." *Ethnology*. Vol. 2, 1963, 40–54.

Elwood, Douglas J. *Churches and Sects in the Philippines*. Dumaguete City, Philippines, Silliman University, 1968.

———. "Contemporary Churches and Sects in the Philippines." *The Southeast Asia Journal of Theology*. October, 1967, 56–78.

Eslao, Nena B. "Child Rearing Among the Samals of Manubul, Siasi,

Sulu." *Philippine Sociological Review*. Vol. 10, No. 3–4, July–October, 1962, 80–91.

——. "The Developmental Cycle of the Philippine Household in an Urban Setting." *Philippine Sociological Review*. Vol. 14, 1966, 199–208.

Facing Facts in Modern Missions. A symposium. Moody Press, Chicago, 1963.

Flattery, Phyllis. *Aspects of Divination in Northern Philippines*. Research Series No. 6, Philippine Studies Program, Department of Anthropology, University of Chicago, June, 1968.

Flores, Plura Medina. "Children's Perception—A Reflection of Man's and Society's Value System." *Culture and Personality*. Edited by F. Landa Jocano. Filipino Cultural Heritage Lecture Series No. 3, Gem Publications, Philippine Women's University, Manila, 1966.

——. "Immanent Justice in Filipino Children and Youth." *Philippine Sociological Review*. Vol. 12, No. 3–4, July–October, 1964, 151–59.

Folkmar, D. "Social Institutions of the Tinglayan Igorot." Typescript copies. University of Chicago Philippine Studies Center, 1906.

Foster, George M. "Confradia and Compadrazgo in Spain and Spanish America." *Southwestern Journal of Anthropology*. Vol. 9, Spring, 1953, 10ff.

——. "Peasant Society and the Image of Limited Good." *American Anthropologist*. Vol. 67, 1965, 293–315.

——. "A Second Look at Limited Good." *Anthropological Quarterly*. Vol. 45, No. 2, April, 1972, 57–63.

Fox, Robert B. "The Family and Society in the Rural Philippines." *Science Review*. National Science Development Board, Manila, April, 1961, 1–5.

——. "The Filipino Family in Perspective," in *Saturday Parade Magazine* of *The Evening News*, Manila, October 15, 1960.

——. "General Character of the Society," in *Area Handbook on the Philippines*. Supervising editor, Fred Eggan and others. The University of Chicago for Human Relations Area Files, 1956, Vol. 1, 1–10.

——. "Language," in *Area Handbook on the Philippines*. Supervising editor, Fred Eggan and others. The University of Chicago for Human Relations Area Files. 1956, Vol. 1, 321–355.

——. "Social Organization," in *Area Handbook on the Philippines*. Supervising editor, Fred Eggan and others. The University of Chicago for Human Relations Area Files, 1956, Vol. 1, 413–470.

Frake, Charles O. "The Diagnosis of Disease among the Subanum of Mindanao." *American Anthropologist*, Vol. 63, 1961, 113–132. Reprinted in Dell Hymes, *Language in Culture and Society*. Harper and Row, Publishers, New York, 1964, 193–211.

———. "The Eastern Subanun of Mindanao," in G.P. Murdock, ed. *Social Structure in Southeast Asia*. Quadrangle Books, Viking Fund Publications in Anthropology, Chicago, Illinois, 1961, 51–64.

———. "A Structural Description of Subanum 'Religious Behavior,'" in Ward H. Goodenough, ed. *Explorations in Cultural Anthropology: Essays in Honor of George Peter Murdock*. McGraw-Hill Book Company, New York, 1964, 111–129.

Freeman, John. "The Concept of Kindred." *Journal of the Royal Anthropological Institute*. Vol. 91, No. 2, July-December, 1961, 192–220.

Fresnoza, Florencio P. *Essentials of the Philippine Educational System*. Revised edition. Albina House, Manila, 1957.

Friend, Theodore. *Between Two Empires*. Yale University Press, New Haven, 1965, 312 pp. (An historical work that also gives cultural insights, this study focuses on the relationship of the Philippines with the United States and Japan during the years 1929–1946.)

Fujimoto, Isao. "The Social Complexity of Philippine Towns and Cities." *Solidarity*. Vol. 3, No. 5, May, 1968.

Gonzales, Pilar. "Changes in the Filipino Family." *Philippine Sociological Review*. Vol. 3, No. 2, April, 1955, 15–17.

Gonzalez, Mary A. "The Ilongo Kinship System and Terminology." *Philippine Sociological Review*. January, 1965, 23–31.

Gorospe, Vitaliano R. "Christian Renewal of Filipino Values," in *Split-Level Christianity (and) Christian Renewal of Filipino Values*. Ateneo University Press, Quezon City, 1966, 19–59. (The author points out the need of renewal and suggests that Filipino values are not obstructions but rather provide the matrix or potential for the maximum development of Christian values.)

Gowing, Peter G. "Christianity in the Philippines Yesterday and Today." *Silliman Journal*. Dumaguete City, Vol. 12, No. 2, April, 1965, 109–51.

———. *Islands Under the Cross*. National Council of Churches in the Philippines, Manila, 1967, 286 pp.

——— and William Henry Scott, eds. *Acculturation in the Philippines: Essays on Changing Societies*. New Day Publishers, Quezon City, 1971.

Grossholtz, Jean. *Politics in the Philippines*. Little, Brown and Co., Boston, 1964.

Grunder, Garel A. *The Philippines and the United States*. University of Oklahoma Press, Norman, Oklahoma, 1951, 315 pp.

144

————. "The Philippine Temperament." *Six Perspectives of the Philippines*. The Bookmark, Manila, 1968.

————, et al. *The Psychology of Modernization in the Rural Philippines*. IPC Papers, No. 8, Ateneo de Manila University Press, Quezon City, 1970, 145 pp.

————, ed. *Six Perspectives on the Philippines*. Bookmark Inc., Manila, 1968.

———— and Fortunata M. Azores. "Philippine Interpersonal Behavior Patterns." *Modernization: Its Impact in the Philippines III*. IPC Papers, No. 6, Ateneo de Manila University Press, Quezon City, 1968, 3–63. (An examination of some recurring interpersonal behavior patterns in an attempt to identify typical person-to-person relationships and the ways which Filipinos use to resolve conflicting demands.)

———— and Pepita Jimenez Jacobs. *Child Rearing and Personality Development in the Philippines*, The Pennsylvania State University Press, University Park, Pennsylvania, 1966.

————, Frank Lynch and Walden F. Bello. *Modernization: Its Impact in the Philippines II*. IPC Papers, No. 5. Ateneo de Manila University Press, Quezon City, 1967, 172 pp. (This volume contains a description of the fishing industry of Estancia, Iloilo; a survey of Filipino child-rearing practices; a review of past research on altruism; and a report on the "cognitive maps" of natives of Marilao, Bulacan.)

Grunlan, Stephen A. and Marvin K. Mayers. *Cultural Anthropology: a Christian Perspective*. Zondervan, Grand Rapids, 1979.

Guzman, Raul P. de. *Patterns in Decision-Making: Case Studies in Public Administration*. Graduate School of Public Administration, University of the Philippines, Manila, 1963.

Guerrero, Sylvia H. "An Analysis of Husband-Wife Roles among Filipino Professionals at U.P. Los Baños Campus." *Philippine Sociological Review*. Vol. 13, No. 4, October, 1965, 275–81.

———— and Gelia T. Castillo. "A Preliminary Study on Alienation." *Philippine Sociological Review*. Vol. 14, No. 2, April, 1966, 85–93.

Guthrie, George M. "Cultural Preparation for the Philippines." Edited by Robert B. Textor. *Cultural Frontiers of the Peace Corps*. The Massachusetts Institute of Technology Press, Mass., 1966.

————. *The Filipino Child and Philippine Society*. Philippine Normal College Press, Manila, 1961.

————. "Impressions of Ifugao Health and Social Activities." Research Bulletin No. 42, Department of Psychology, Pennsylvania State University, 1964.

Hare, Paul A. "Cultural Differences in Performance in Communication Networks Among Filipino, African, and American Students," in

Modernization: Its Impact in the Philippines IV. Quezon City, 1969, 24–45. (A cross-cultural small-group experiment involving the "circle," the "chain," the "Y," and the "wheel" types of communication networks.)

—— and Rachel T. Hare. "Social Correlates of Autonomy Among University Students in the Philippines, United States, and Africa," in *Modernization: Its Impact in the Philippines III*. IPC Papers, No. 6. Ateneo de Manila University Press, Quezon City, 1968, 92–104. (A cross-cultural social psychology study in which an autonomy scale and a social-background questionnaire were administered to university students in varying cultures.)

—— and Dean Peabody. "Attitude Content and Agreement Set in the Autonomy Scale for Filipino, American and African University Students," in *Modernization: Its Impact in the Philippines III*. IPC Papers, No. 6, Ateneo de Manila Press, Quezon City, 1968, 105–113.

Hare, Rachel. "Autonomy, Dependency, and Problem Solving in Filipino Children," in *Modernization: Its Impact in the Philippines IV*. IPC Papers, No. 7. Ateneo de Manila University Press, Quezon City, 1969, 46–59.

——. "Cultural Differences in the Use of Guilt and Shame in Child Rearing: a Review of the Research on the Philippines and other non-Western Societies," in *Modernization: Its Impact in the Philippines II*. IPC Papers, No. 5. Ateneo de Manila University Press, Quezon City, 1967, 35–76.

Hart, Donn Vorhis. *The Cebuan Filipino Dwelling in Caticugan: Its Construction and Cultural Aspects*. Southeast Asia Studies, Cultural Report Series, Yale University, New Haven, 1959.

——. *The Philippine Plaza Complex*. Southeast Asia Studies, Cultural Report Series, Yale University, New Haven, 1955.

Hartoko, Dick. "The Philippines: A Coca Colonized Country." *Solidarity*. Manila, Vol. 3, No. 5, May, 1968.

Hayden, Joseph Ralston. *The Philippines, A Study in National Development*, The Macmillan Company, New York, 1942, 984 pp. (A detailed study of the Philippine's development in the area of politics and government up until 1935.)

Herrmann, Carol B. *New Discoveries From Cross-Cultural Confrontation: A Missionary Anthropological Study of Encounters With a Distinct Culture—The Philippines*. m.s., Wheaton College, Wheaton, Illinois, 1970.

Hessel, Eugene A. *The Religious Thought of José Rizal*. Philippine Education Company, Manila, 1961, 289 pp. (Rizal, a Filipino hero, openly criticized the Spanish colonial system in the late eighteen hundreds.)

Himes, Ronald S. "The Bontoc Kinship System." *Philippine Sociological Review*. Vol. 12, 1964, 159–172.

———. "Cognitive Mapping in the Tagalog Area (II)," in *Modernization: Its Impact in the Philippines II*. IPC Papers, No. 5. Ateneo de Manila University Press, Quezon City, 1967, 125–168.

Hollnsteiner, Mary R. "Commentary on 'Barrio Institutions and Their Economic Implications' by Agaton P. Pal." *Philippine Sociological Review*. Vol. 7, No. 1–2, January-April, 1959, 63–64.

———. *The Dynamics of Power in a Philippine Municipality*. Community Development Research Council, University of the Philippines, Quezon City, 1963, 227 pp. (An excellent study of the struggle for power that takes place in a lowland community in the Philippines. The focus of this pioneering work is on alliance groups and the importance of kinship.)

———. "A Lowland Philippine Municipality in Transition." *Practical Anthropology*. Vol. 8, No. 2, March-April, 1961, 54–62. (Focus of this article is on a lowland nonpagan community in Bulacan, a province just north of Manila. Hulo, as the author named the municipality, is also dealt with in Hollnsteiner's *The Dynamics of Power in a Philippine Municipality*.)

———. "The Lowland Philippine Alliance System in Municipal Politics." *Philippine Sociological Review*. Vol. 11, No. 3, July, 1962, 167–171.

———. *Manila Microcosm: Leadership, Belonging, and Viewpoints in a Tondo Neighborhood*. Institute of Philippine Culture, Ateneo de Manila University Press, Quezon City, forthcoming IPC publication. (This study deals with life in Tondo, a lower-income neighborhood of Manila.)

———. "Modernization and the Challenge to the Filipino Family." *The Filipino Christian Family in a Changing Society*. Christian Family Movement, Manila, 1965, 10–20.

———. "A Note to Management on Traditional Filipino Values in Business Enterprises: The Lumber Company as a Case Study." *Philippine Studies*. Vol. 13, No. 2, April, 1965, 350–54.

———. "Philippine Values." Unpublished notes from class lectures. Mimeographed.

———. "Reciprocity in the Lowland Philippines," in *Four Readings on Philippine Values*. IPC Papers, No. 2, third edition, revised and enlarged. Ateneo de Manila University Press, Quezon City, 1970, 65–88. (A discussion of contractual, quasi-contractual and *utang na loob* types of reciprocity.)

————. "Social Control and Filipino Personality." *Philippine Sociological Review*, Vol. 11, No. 3–4, July-October, 1963.

————. "Some Principles of Culture Change and Their Relation to the Philippines." *Philippine Sociological Review*. Vol. 11, No. 1, January, 1958, 1–7.

————. "The Urbanization of Metropolitan Manila," in *Modernization: Its Impact in the Philippines IV*. IPC Papers, No. 7. Ateneo de Manila University Press, Quezon City, 1969, 147–174.

Hunt, Chester L. "Social Distance in the Philippines." *Sociology and Social Research*. Vol. 40, March, 1956, 253–60.

————, et al. *Sociology in the Philippine Setting*. Revised edition. Phoenix Publishing House, Quezon City, 1963, 373 pp. (An elementary introduction to sociology with its focus on the Philippine sociocultural setting.)

———— and Socorro C. Espiritu, eds. *Social Foundations of Community Development: Readings on the Philippines*. Manila, 1964, 684 pp.

———— and Thomas R. McHale. "Education, Attitudinal Change and Philippine Economic Development." *Philippine Sociological Review*. Vol. 13, No. 3, July, 1965, 127–39.

Ison, Rosalinda. *Developing a Filipino Christian Camping Philosophy*. m.s., Masters thesis for Conservative Baptist Theological Seminary, Denver, 1969.

Jenks, A.E. *The Bontoc Igorot*. Philippine Islands Ethnological Survey Publications, Manila, Vol. 1, 1905.

Jennings, George J. "The Tasaday and the Problem of Social Evolution." *Journal of the American Scientific Affiliation*. Vol. 24, No. 2, June, 1972, 58–63.

Jocano, F. Landa. "Agricultural Rituals in a Philippine Barrio." *Philippine Sociological Review*. Vol. 2, No. 1–2, January-April, 1967, 48–56.

————. "Cultural Context of Folk Medicine: Some Philippine Cases." *Philippine Sociological Review*. January, 1966, 40–48.

————. "Conversion and the Patterning of Christian Experience in Malitbog, Central Panay, Philippines." *Philippine Sociological Review*. Vol. 13, No. 2, April, 1965, 96–119.

————. "Filipino Social Structure and Value System." *Structure and Value Orientation*. Filipino Cultural Heritage Lecture Series, No. 2. Gem Publications, Philippine Women's University, Manila, 1966.

————. *Growing up in a Philippine Barrio*. Holt, Rinehart and Winston, New York, 1969, 121 pp. (A case study in education and an ethnography, this book presents the life cycle of farmers in Malitbog, a small peasant barrio located in the central region of Panay island.

Emphasis is placed upon techniques of cultural learning and transmission in the community.)

———. "Language and Socialization: Some Comments on the Process of Cultural Learning." *Culture and Personality*. Filipino Cultural Heritage Lecture Series, No. 3. Gem Publications, Philippine Women's University, Manila, 1966.

———. "Notes on Philippine Divinities." *Asian Studies*. University of the Philippines, Vol. 6, No. 2, August, 1968, 169–182.

———. *Our Living Past: The Philippines from 250,000 B.C. to 1,500 A.D.* Phoenix Publishing House, Quezon City, 1963, 75 pp.

———. "Rethinking Filipino Cultural Heritage." *Lipunan*. Vol. 1, 1964, 53–71.

———. "Rethinking 'Smooth Interpersonal Relations.' " *Philippine Sociological Review*. Vol. 14, No. 4, 1966, 282–91.

———. *Structure and Value Orientation*. Filipino Cultural Heritage Lecture Series, No. 2. Gem Publications, Philippine Women's University, Manila, 1966. (Note especially Jocano's article on "Filipino Social Structure and Value System.")

———. "The Structure of Social Relations and Its Implications for Social Change: A Conceptual Analysis." *Philippine Sociological Review*. Vol. 11, 1963, 206–215.

———. *Sulod Society: A Study in Kinship System and Social Organization of a Mountain People of Central Pandy*. University of the Philippines Press, Quezon City, 1968.

———. *The Traditional World of Malitbog: A Study of Community Development and Culture Change in a Philippine Barrio*. Community Development Research Council, Quezon City, 1968. (A discussion of the difficulties facing a program of change and the agent of change in a Philippine barrio.)

———. "Variations in Philippine Culture: A Western Visayan Case Study." *Southeast Asia Quarterly*. Vol. 1, No. 1, 1966.

Kast, Edward L. "Comments on Church, Plaza and Market Place." *Practical Anthropology*. Vol. 10, 1963, 175–178.

Kaut, Charles. "Utang na Loob: A System of Contractual Obligation Among Tagalogs." *Southwestern Journal of Anthropology*. Vol. 17, No. 3, 1961, 256–272.

Keesing, Felix M. "Cultural Trends in the Philippines." *Far Eastern Quarterly*. Vol. 9, 1945, 102–18.

———. *The Ethnohistory of Northern Luzon*. Stanford University Press, Stanford, California, 1962, 362 pp.

———. "The Isneg: Shifting Cultivators of the Northern Philippines." *Southwestern Journal of Anthropology*. Vol. 18, 1962, 1–19.

––––––. "Some Notes on Bontok Social Organization, Northern Philippines." *American Anthropologist*. Vol. 51, 1949, 578–601.

––––––. *Taming Philippine Headhunters: A Study of Government and of Cultural Change in Northern Luzon*. Stanford University Press, Stanford, California, 1934, 288 pp.

Keith, Agness Newton. *Barefeet in the Palace*. Little, Brown and Company, Boston, 1955, 370 pp. (An account of daily life in the Manila area as observed by a North American woman writer during the term of Magsaysay.)

Kiefer, Thomas M. "Institutionalized Friendship and Warfare Among the Tausug of Jolo." *Ethnology*. Vol. 7, July, 1968, 225–44.

––––––. "Reciprocity and Revenge in the Philippines: Some Preliminary Remarks about the Tausug of Jolo." *Philippine Sociological Review*. Vol. 16, No. 3–4, 1968, 124–31.

Kietzman, Dale W. and William A. Smalley. "The Missionary's Role in Culture Change." *Practical Anthropology*, Supplement, 1960, 276–281.

King, Louis L. "The Philippines." *Missionary Atlas: A Manual of the Foreign Work of the Christian and Missionary Alliance*. Christian Publications, Inc., Harrisburg, Pennsylvania, 1964, 161–169.

Kraft, Charles H. "Christian Conversion or Cultural Conversion." *Practical Anthropology*. Vol. 10, 1963, 179–187.

Krieger, Herbert William. *Peoples of the Philippines*. The Smithsonian Institute, City of Washington, 1942, 86 pp.

Kroeber, Alfred Louis. "The History of Philippine Civilization as Reflected in Religious Nomenclature." *Anthropological Papers of the American Museum of Natural History*. Vol. 19, No. 2, 1918, 67 pp. (Kroeber finds relationships with the socioreligious systems of the East by analyzing various Filipino languages.)

––––––. "Kinship in the Philippines." *Anthropological Papers of the American Museum of Natural History. Vol. 19, No. 3, 1919, 69–84.*

––––––. *Peoples of the Philippines*. American Museum of Natural History Press, New York, 1928, 245 pp.

Kuhn, Delia and Ferdinand. *The Philippines Yesterday and Today*. Holt, Rinehart and Winston, New York, 1966, 248 pp.

Lambrecht, Francis. "Adoption of Ifugao Local Customs in Christianity." *Philippine Sociological Review*. Vol. 11, 1963, 12–27.

––––––. "Ifugao Custom and the Moral Law." *Philippine Studies*. Vol. 10, No. 2, April, 1962, 275–299.

––––––. "The Mayawyaw Ritual: Rice Culture and Rice Ritual." Publications of the Catholic Anthropological Conference. Vol. 4, No. 1, 1932, 1–167.

———. "The Mayawyaw Ritual: Marriage and Marriage Ritual." Publications of the Catholic Anthropological Conference. Vol. 4, No. 2, 1935, 169–325.

———. "The Mayawyaw Ritual: Death and Death Ritual." Publications of the Catholic Anthropological Conference. Vol. 4, No. 3, 1938, 327–493.

———. "The Mayawyaw Ritual: Property and Property Ritual." Publications of the Catholic Anthropological Conference. Vol. 4, No. 4, 1939, 495–711.

———. "The Mayawyaw Ritual: Go-Betweens and Priests." Publications of the Catholic Anthropological Conference. Vol. 4, No. 5, 1941, 713–754.

———. "Property Laws of Custom Among the Ifugaos." *Silliman Journal*. Vol. 11, 1964, 57–70.

———. "The Religion of the Ifugaos." *Philippine Sociological Review*. Vol. 10, No. 1–2, January-April, 1962, 33–40.

Lande, Carl H. *Leaders, Factions, and Parties: The Structure of Philippine Politics*. Southeast Asia Studies, Monograph Series No. 6, Yale University, 1964.

Landis, R.M. "The Philippines," in *Missionary Atlas*. Christian and Missionary Alliance, New York, 1960.

Laquian, Aprodicio A. *Slums are for People: The Barrio Magsaysay Pilot Project in Urban Community Development*. University of the Philippines, College of Public Administration, Local Government Center, Manila, 1969.

Larson, Donald M. "Church, Plaza, and the Market Place." *Practical Anthropology*. Vol. 10, 1963, 167–174.

Larson, Donald N. "The Philippine Language Scene." *Philippine Sociological Review*. Vol. 11, No. 1–2, January-April, 1963, 4–12.

Laubach, Frank Charles. *The People of the Philippines*. George H. Doran Company, New York, 1925.

Leeder, Leo L. "A Survey of Pagan Tribes in the Philippines and of Missionary Efforts Toward their Evangelization." An unpublished M.A. thesis, Columbia Bible College, 1956.

Le Roy, James A. *The Americans in the Philippines*. Vol. 1, Houghton Mifflin Company, Boston, 1914.

Levi-Strauss, Claude. "The Principle of Reciprocity." *Sociological Theory: A Book of Readings*. Lewis Coser and Bernard Rosenberg, eds. The Macmillan Company, New York, 1957, 84–94.

Lieban, Richard W. *Cebuano Sorcery: Malign Magic in the Philippines*. University of California Press, Berkeley, 1967.

————. "Sorcery, Illness, and Social Control in a Philippine Municipality."*Southwestern Journal of Anthropology*. Vol. 16, 1960, 127–143.

Lim, Estefania, Aldaba. "Dynamics of Filipino Personality." *Culture and Personality*. Filipino Cultural Heritage Lecture Series, No. 3. Gem Publications, Philippine Women's University, Manila, 1966.

Lim, Manuel. *Shortcomings of the Philippine Educational System, Remedial Measures Adopted and Proposed Solutions*. Department of Education, Manila, 1959.

Llamzon, Teodoro A. *The IPC Guide to Tagalog, Ilocano, Ibanag*. Ateneo de Manila University Press, Quezon City, 130 pp. (A pocket guide designed for the foreigner visiting the Philippines.)

————. "The Subgrouping of Philippine Languages." *Philippine Sociological Review*. Vol. 14, No. 3, July, 1966, 145–150.

Loewen, Jacob A. "The Christian Encounter with Culture." *World Vision Magazine*. January, 1967, 13ff.

————. "Christian Encounter with Needs People Feel." *World Vision Magazine*. February, 1967, 13ff.

————. "Overcoming Resistance;" *World Vision Magazine*. March, 1967, 11ff.

————. "Reciprocity in Identification." *Practical Anthropology*. Vol. 11, 1964, 144–145.

———— and Anne Loewen. "Role, Self-Image and Missionary Communication." *Practical Anthropology*. Vol. 14, 1967, 145–160.

Loscano, Pociano and Lauro Quinto. *History and Cultural Life of Lipa City*. Mimeo., n.d.

Lowie, R.H. "Kinship." *Encyclopedia of the Social Sciences*. Vol. 3, 1931, 568–572. (A clear presentation of kinship systems.)

Lumbera, Bienvenido. "Literary Notes on the Filipino Personality." *Philippine Sociological Review*. Vol. 11, No. 3–4, July-October, 1963, 163–206.

Luzbetak, Louis J. *The Church and Cultures: An Applied Anthropology for Religious Workers*. Divine Word Publications, Techny, Illinois, 1963.

————. "Toward an Applied Missionary Anthropology." *Practical Anthropology*. Vol. 10, 1963, 199–208.

Lynch, Frank. "The Anatomy of Clannishness." Lecture delivered March 5, 1969 at the San Miguel Auditorium, Maksti. (This was the ninth lecture in a series entitled "The Foundations and Character of Filipino Society," sponsored by the Research Foundation in Philippine Anthropology and Archaeology, Inc.)

————. "The Conjugal Bond Where the Philippines Changes." *Philippine*

Sociological Review. Vol. 7, No. 3–4, July-October, 1960, 48–51.

———. "Continuities in Philippine Social Class." *Historical Bulletin.* Vol. 6, No. 1, March, 1962, 40–51.

———, Compiler. *Four Readings on Philippine Values.* IPC Papers, No. 2, Ateneo de Manila University Press, Quezon City, 1962. (An invaluable introduction to the study of Filipino culture. Social acceptance, reciprocity, Manila values, and the origins of the Filipino manufacturing entrepreneur are all discussed.)

———, Compiler. "Organized Religion," in *Area Handbook on the Philippines.* University of Chicago for Human Relations Area Files. 1956, Vol. 2, 471–686. (An objective survey analysis of religion in the Philippines. Note especially the section on "Catholicism.")

———, et al. *The Philippines Peace Corps Survey Final Report.* Social Science Research Institute, Honolulu, 1966.

———. "A Philippine Village: Report from the Field." *Anthropology Tomorrow.* Vol. 6, No. 2, 1958, 13–29.

———. "Significance of the Nature of the Philippine Community in Community Development Programs." *Asia: Community Development in the Philippines.* Southern Illinois University, Carbondale, Illinois, 1960, 13–26.

———. "Social Acceptance Reconsidered," in *Four Readings on Philippine Values.* IPC Papers, No. 2, Ateneo de Manila University Press, Quezon City, 1968, 1–63.

———. *Social Class in a Bikol Town.* University of Chicago, Chicago, 1959. (A study done in 1956–1958 in which the social stratification system of a Philippine rural community was examined.)

———, ed. *Sulu's People and Their Art.* IPC Papers, No. 3. Ateneo de Manila University Press, Quezon City, 1963, 66 pp. (Contains a discussion of the social organization of the Taosug, Samal, and Badjaw—Sulu's main ethnic groups; also reports on a reconnaissance of Sulu art.)

———, ed. "Town Fiesta: An Anthropologist's View." *Philippines International.* Vol. 4, No. 6, June, 1962, 4–11, 26–27.

———, ed. "Trends Report of Studies in Social Stratification and Social Mobility in the Philippines." *East Asian Cultural Studies.* Vol. 4, No. 1–4, March, 1965, 163–191. (A comparative survey of the available materials on social stratification and social mobility in the Philippines.)

——— and Ronald S. Himes. "Cognitive Mapping in the Tagalog Area," in *Modernization: Its Impact in the Philippines.* IPC Papers, No. 4. Ateneo de Manila University Press, Quezon City, 1967, 9–52.

——— and Mary R. Hollnsteiner, eds. *Northeast Luzon: The Place and the*

People. IPC Regional Handbook Series. Ateneo de Manila University Press, Quezon City, 1964, 265 pp.

────── and ──────. "Sixty Years of Philippine Ethnology." *Science Review*, Vol. 2, No. 11, November, 1961, 1–5.

────── and ──────. *Understanding the Philippines and America: A Study of Cultural Trends*. Institute of Philippines Culture Publications, Ateneo de Manila University Press, Quezon City, 1966. (Insights into Filipino behavior gained through an anthropological analysis of Tagalog dialogues.)

────── and ──────. *Understanding the Philippines and Americans: A Study of Cultural Trends*. Revised. Institute of Philippine Culture Publication, Ateneo de Manila University Press, Quezon City, 1966, 436 pp.

────── and Perla Q. Makil. "Sociological Surveys in the Rural Philippines: Some Suggestions for Interviewers," in *Modernization: Its Impact in the Philippines*. IPC Papers, No. 4. Ateneo de Manila University Press, Quezon City, 1967, 106–128.

Lynip, G. Louise. *On Good Ground: Missionary Stories from the Philippines*. Wm. B. Eerdmans Publishing Company, Grand Rapids, Michigan, 1946, 149 pp.

Macaraig, Serafin E. *Introduction to Sociology*. University of the Philippines, Manila, 1948. (An introductory textbook containing Philippine illustrations.)

McBride, Clarence. "The Social Responsibility of the Rural Church." *Philippine Sociological Review*. Vol. 12, No. 1–2, January-April, 1964, 129–135.

McGavran, Donald Anderson. *The Bridges of God*. Friendship Press, New York, 1955.

──────. *Multiplying Churches in the Philippines*. United Church of Christ in the Philippines, Manila, 1958.

──────. *Understanding Church Growth*. Wm. B. Eerdmans Publishing Company, Grand Rapids, Michigan, 1970.

McHale, Thomas R. "A Modern Corporation Looks at the Philippine Economy and Society in Transition." *Philippine Sociological Review*. October, 1966, 226–231.

Madigan, Francis. "The Farmer Said No: A Study of Background Factors Associated with Dispositions to Cooperate with or be Resistant to Community Development Projects." Diliman, Community Development Research Council, University of the Philippines, Quezon City, Study Series 14.

──────. "Predicting Receptivity to Community Development Innovations." *Current Anthropology*. Vol. 3, No. 2, April, 1962, 207–208.

Malinowski, Bronislaw. "Reciprocity and Obligation," in *Man and Society*. Jerome Manis and Samuel Clark, eds. Macmillan, New York, 1960.

Mandoriao, Jose. *The Hour Before Sunset*. The Higley Press, Butler, Indiana, 1957.

Manuel, E. Arsenio. *Chinese Elements in the Tagalog Language*. Filipiniana Publications, Manila, 1948, 139 pp. (A scholarly study of words in Tagalog that show the influence of Chinese.)

Manuud, Antonio G., ed. *Brown Heritage: Essays on Philippine Cultural Tradition and Literature*. Ateneo de Manila University Press, Quezon City, 1967.

Mayers, Marvin K. *Christianity Confronts Culture: A Strategy for Cross-Cultural Evangelism*. Zondervan, Grand Rapids, Michigan, 1974.

_____.*A Look at Latin American Lifestyles*. Summer Institute of Linguistics Museum of Anthropology, Publication 2, Dallas, Texas, 1976, 80–83.

_____, Lawrence Richards, and Robert Webber, *Reshaping Evangelical Higher Education*. Zondervan Publishing House, Grand Rapids, 1972.

Mednick, Melvin. *Encampment of the Lake: The Social Organization of a Moslem-Philippine (Moro) People*. Chicago, Philippine Studies Program, Department of Anthropology, University of Chicago, 1965.

Mellnik, Stephen Michael. *Philippine Diary, 1939–1945*. Forward by Carlos Romulo. Van Nostrand, 1969, 316 pp.

Merk, Frederick. *Manifest Destiny and Mission in American History: A Reinterpretation*. Vintage Books, New York, 1963, 265 pp.

Minturn, Leigh and W.W. Lambert. *Mothers of Six Cultures*. Wiley, New York, 1965. (Controlled comparisons of small samples in Mexico, Okinawa, Philippines, India, East Africa, and New England.)

Mintz, Sidney W. and Eric R. Wolf. "An Analysis of Ritual Co-Parenthood (Compadrazgo)." *Southwestern Journal of Anthropology*. Vol. 6,1950, 341–368.

Montgomery, Jim. *New Testament Fire in the Philippines*. C-Grip, FEBC Marshburn Press, 1972.

Munoz, Alfredo. *The Filipinos in America*. Mountain View Publishers, Los Angeles, 1971. (An analysis of present-day Filipinos living in the United States.)

Murdock, George Peter. *Social Structure in Southeast Asia*. Wenner Gren Foundation for Anthropological Research, Inc., New York, 1960.

Nadel, S.F. "A Study of Shamanism in the Nuba Mountains." *Journal of the Royal Anthropological Institute*. Vol. 76, 1946, 25–37.

Nelson, Raymond. *The Philippines*. Walker and Company, New York, 1968. (A concise survey book tracing the history of the Philippines from prehistory to present day.)

Nida, Eugene. "Cultural Difference and Communications." *Practical Anthropology*. Vol. 10, 1963, 241–258.

———. *God's Word in Man's Language*. Harper and Row, New York, 1952.

———. "Identification, a Major Problem of Modern Missions." *Practical Anthropology*. Vol. 2, 1955, 90–95.

———. *Message and Mission: The Communication of the Christian Faith*. Harper and Row, New York, 1960.

———. *Religion Across Cultures*. Harper and Row, New York, 1968.

———. "The Role of Cultural Anthropology in Christian Missions." *Practical Anthropology*. Vol. 6, 1959, 110–116.

Niebuhr, Reinhold. *Moral Man and Immoral Society*. Scribner's Sons Publishers, New York, 1932, 99–103.

Nimkoff, Meyer F. *Comparative Family Systems*. Houghton Mifflin Company, Boston, 1965.

Nimmo, H.A. "Bajau Sex and Reproduction." *Ethnology*. Vol. 9, July, 1970, 251–262.

Noble, Lowell L. "Can St. Paul's Methods Be Ours?" *Practical Anthropology*. Vol. 8, 1961, 180–185.

Nurge, Ethel. "Economic Functions of the Child in the Rural Philippines." *Philippine Sociological Review*. Vol. 4, No. 1, January, 1956, 7–11.

———. *Life in the Leyte Village*. University of Washington Press, Seattle, 1965, 157 pp. (An analysis of life in a Philippine village of Leyte around 1955–56. Focuses upon the mother-child relationship and its effect on personality.)

Nydegger, William F. and Corinne Nydegger. *Tarong: An Ilocos Barrios in the Philippines*. Six Culture Series: Vol. 6. John Wiley and Sons, 1966, 180 pp. (Describes life and parent-child relationships among the Ilokanos.)

Oberg, Kalerva. "Cultural Shock: Adjustment to New Cultural Environments." *Practical Anthropology*. Vol. 7, 1960, 177–182.

Osias, Camilo. *The Filipino Way of Life: The Pluralized Philosophy*. Ginn and Company, New York, 1940.

———. *Jose Rizal: His Life and Times*. Oscal Educational Publishers, Manila, 1948.

——— and Avelina Lorenzana. *Evangelical Christianity in the Philippines*. The United Brethren Publishing House, Dayton, Ohio, 1931, 240 pp.

Pacana, Honesto C. "Notes on a Filipino Role of Conduct: Non-Interference." *Philippine Sociological Review*. Vol. 6, No. 1, January, 1958, 29–30.

Pacyaya, Alfredo G. "Changing Customs of Marriage, Death, and Burial among the Sagada Igorots." *Practical Anthropology*. Vol. 8, 1961, 125–133.

Padilla, Sinforoso G. and Estefania Aldaba-Lim. "Psychology in the Philippines." *Science Review*, Vol. 2, No. 11, November, 1961, 6–10.

Pal, Agaton. "Aspects of Lowland Philippine Social Structure." *Philippine Sociological Review*, January, 1966, 31–40.

_____. "Channels of Communication with the Barrio People." *Philippine Journal of Public Administration*. Vol. I, No. 2, April, 1957, 145–149.

_____. "A Philippine Barrio." *Journal of East Asiatic Studies*. Vol. 5, No. 4, 1956.

_____. "A Philippine Barrio: A Study of Social Organization in Relation to Planned Cultural Change." Unpublished Doctoral Dissertation. Cornell University, Ithaca, New York, 1956, 400 pp.

_____. *The Resources, Levels of Living, and Aspirations of Rural in Negros Orientals*. Community Development Research Council, University of the Philippines, Quezon City, 1963, 429 pp.

Peabody, Dean. "Group Judgments in the Philippines: Their Evaluative and Descriptive Aspects," in *Modernization: Its Impact in the Philippines III*. IPC Papers, No. 6. Ateneo de Manila University Press, Quezon City, 1968, 114–128.

Pecson, Geronima T., and Maria Racelis, eds. *Tales of American Teachers in the Philippines*. Carmel and Bauermann, Manila, 1959.

Phelan, John Leddy. *The Hispanization of the Philippines: Spanish Aims and Filipino Responses 1565–1700*. University of Wisconsin Press, Madison, 1959, 218 pp. (A very good discussion of the effects of Spanish rule on the Filipino sociocultural system.)

Pitts, Joseph S. *Missions to the Philippines*. Beacon Hill Press, Kansas City, Missouri, 1956, 127 pp.

Poethig, Richard P. *Philippine Social Issues from a Christian Perspective*. United Church of Christ in the Philippines, Manila, 1963, 222 pp. (An approach to Christian ethics within the sociocultural setting of the Philippines.)

_____. "Summary of a Study on Background of Protestant Seminarians." *Philippine Sociological Review*. Vol. 13, No. 2, April, 1965, 85–90.

Pratt, Julius W. *Expansionists of 1898: The Acquisition of Hawaii and the Spanish Islands*. Baltimore, 1936.

_____. "Family Size and Expectations in Manila." *Saint Louis Quarterly*. Vol. 5, No. 1–2, 153–184.

Quisumbing, Lourdes. "Characteristic Features of the Cebuano Family

Life." *Philippine Sociological Review*. Vol. 11, No. 1–2, January-April, 1963, 135–141.

Radcliffe-Brown, A.R. "The Study of Kinship Systems," in *Structure and Function in Primitive Society*. The Free Press, New York, 1952. (A classic work on kinship.)

Ravenholt, Albert J. *The Philippines: A Young Republic on the Move*. D. Van Nostrand Company, Princeton, New Jersey, 1962, 204 pp. (An account of Philippine history in relation to present problems.)

Reid, Lawrence. "Comment on 'The Acceptance of Ifugao Customs in Christianity.'" *Philippine Sociological Review*. 1963, Vol. 11, 28–31.

———. "Ritual and Ceremony in Mountain Province." *Philippine Sociological Review*. 1961, Vol. 9, 1–82.

Renich, Fred. "First-Term Objectives." *Evangelical Missions Quarterly*. Vol. 3, 1967, 209–217.

Reyburn, William D. "Crossing Cultural Frontiers." *Practical Anthropology*. Vol. 15, November-December, 1968, 249–257.

———. "The Missionary and Cultural Diffusion." *Practical Anthropology*. Vol. 5, 1958, 262–275.

———. "The Missionary and the Evolution of Culture." *Practical Anthropology*. Vol. 4, 1951, 238–244.

Reynolds, Harriet R. "The Filipino Family in its Cultural Setting." *Practical Anthropology*. Vol. 9, 1962, 223–234.

Rice, Delbert. "Developing an Indigenous Hymnody." *Practical Anthropology*. Vol. 18, May, 1971, 19–113. (Deals with missions and music in the Philippine Islands.)

———. "Evangelism and Decision-Making Process." *Practical Anthropology*. Vol. 16, November, 1969, 264–273. (Evangelistic work in the Philippines.)

———. "Indigenous Wedding Ceremony." *Evangelical Missions Quarterly*. Vol. 7, Spring, 1971, 151–153. (Indigenous churches in the Philippines.)

———. "Local Church Government among the Ikalahan." *Practical Anthropology*. Vol. 19, March-April, 1972, 49–58. (Deals with the Ikalahan of northern Luzon, Philippines.)

Rich, J.A. "Religious Acculturation in the Philippines." *Practical Anthropology*. Vol. 17, September, 1970, 197–209.

Riggs, Fred W. "A Model for the Study of Philippine Social Structure." *Philippine Sociological Review*. Vol. 8, No. 3, July, 1959, 1–32.

Rizal, José. *The Lost Eden*. Greenwood Press Publishers, New York, 1886, 1968, 407 pp. (This novel, by showing the faults and problems of Spanish rule in the late 1800's, had a great influence on the Philippine struggle for independence. This account of Filipino life was one of the reasons for Rizal's execution.)

———. *The Reign of Greed (El Filibusterismo).* (Translated by Charles E. Derbyshire from the original Spanish.) Philippine Education Company, Manila, 1956.

Roberts, Walter N. *The Filipino Church.* The Foreign Missionary Society and The Woman's Missionary Association, United Brethren in Christ, Dayton, Ohio, 1936.

Roosevelt, Nicholas. *The Philippines: A Treasure and a Problem.* J.H. Sears and Company, Inc., New York, 1926, 315 pp. (An analysis of U.S. role in Philippines as it was perceived in 1926. A rather biased account in the sense of a "superior America" tone throughout; but it does give insight into the atmosphere of the United States at that time.)

Roy, David P., Frank Lynch and Thomas Maretzki. "The Philippines Peace Corps Survey Final Report," in *Modernization: Its Impact in the Philippines.* IPC Papers, No. 4. Ateneo de Manila University Press, Quezon City, 1967. 87–106. (A condensed version of the 1964–66 Philippines Peace Corps Survey by Frank Lynch, et al.)

Saito, Shiro. *Preliminary Bibliography of Philippine Ethnography.* Institute of Philippine Culture and the Rizal Library, Ateneo de Manila University Press, Quezon City, forthcoming IPC publication.

Sanders, Albert J. *The Evangelical Ministry in the Philippines and its Future.* Union Theological Seminary, National Council of Churches in the Philippines, Manila, 1964, 70 pp.

———. *A Protestant View of the Iglesia ni Cristo.* Philippine Federation of Christian Churches, Quezon City, 1962, 72 pp.

Scaff, Alvin H. *The Philippine Answer to Communism.* Stanford University Press, Stanford, 1955, 165 pp.

Scheans, Daniel J. "The Ilocano: Marriage and the Land." *Philippine Sociological Review.* Vol. 13, No. 1, January, 1965, 57–62.

Schusky, Ernest L. *Manual for Kinship Analysis.* Studies in Anthropological Method Series, Holt, Rinehart, and Winston, New York, 1965.

Scott, William Henry. "The Apo-Dios Concept in Northern Luzon." *Practical Anthropology.* Vol. 8, 1961, 207–216.

———. "Economic and Material Culture of the Kalingas of Madukayan." *Southwestern Journal of Anthropology.* 1958, Vol. 14, 318–337.

Sibley, Willis E. "Leadership in a Philippine Barrio." *Philippine Journal of Public Administration.* Vol. 1, No. 2, April, 1957, 154–159.

———. "Persistence, Variety and Change in Visayan Social Organization: a Brief Research Report." *Philippine Sociological Review.* Vol. 13, No. 3, 1965.

————. "Social Structure and Planned Change: A Case Study from the Philippines." *Human Organization*. Vol. 19, No. 4, Winter, 1960–1961, 209–211.

Sinco, Vicente G. *Education in Philippine Society*. University of the Philippines, Quezon City, 1959.

Smalley, William A. "Culture Shock, Language Shock, and the Shock of Self-Discovery." *Practical Anthropology*. Vol. 9, 1963, 49–56.

————. "Respect and Ethnocentrism." *Practical Anthropology*, Vol. 5, 1958, 191–194.

Smith, George. "Education," in *Area Handbook on the Philippines*. Fred Eggan, et al., Supervisors. University of Chicago for Human Relations Area Files, 1956, Vol. 2, 745–995.

Smith, Robert Aura. *Philippine Freedom, 1946–1958*. Columbia University Press, New York, 1958, 375 pp.

Snarey, John. *AnthroPAULogist: A Course in Paul-Like Cross-Cultural Personal Relations*. LEE, Leader Education Enterprises, Box 788, Wheaton, Illinois, 1974.

————. *Jesus-Like Relationships: A Small Group Course in Interpersonal Effectiveness*. LEE, Leader Education Enterprises, Box 788, Wheaton, Illinois, 1974.

Spencer, Joseph E. "The Philippines: An Island Borderland," in *Asia East by South*. John Wiley and Sons, New York, 1954, 284–299. (A geography of the Philippines.)

Spindler, George, ed. *Culture and Education: Anthropological Approaches*. Holt, Rinehart and Winston, New York, 1963.

Spottswood, Curran L. *Beyond Cotabato*. Fleming H. Revell Company, Westwood, New Jersey, 1961.

Sta Romana, Julita Reyes. "Membership and the Norm of Discipline in the Iglesia ni Kristo." *Philippine Sociological Review*. Vol. 3, No. 1, January, 1955, 4–14.

Steinberg, David Joel. *Philippine Collaboration in World War II*. Solari-daridad Publishing House, Manila, 1967.

Stone, Richard L. and Joy Marsella. "Mahirap: A Squatter Community in a Manila Suburb," in *Modernization: Its Impact in the Philippines III*. IPC Papers, No. 6. Ateneo de Manila University Press, Quezon City, 1968, 64–91.

————. "Private Transitory Ownership of Public Property: One Key to Understanding Public Behavior: I—The Driving Game," in *Modernization: Its Impact in the Philippines*. IPC Papers, No. 4. Ateneo de Manila University Press, Quezon City, 1967, 53–63.

Stoodley, Bartlett. "Normative Attitudes of Filipino Youth Compared with German and American Youth." *American Sociological Review.* Vol. 22, No. 5, October, 1957, 553–561.

————. "Some Aspects of Tagalog Family Structure." *American Anthropologist.* Vol. 59, No. 2, April, 1957, 236–249.

Stuntz, Homer C. "Past and Present in the Philippines." *The Missionary Review of the World.* July, 1904, 485–493.

Szanton, David L. "Cultural Confrontation in the Philippines." *Cultural Frontiers of the Peace Corps.* Robert Textor, ed. The Massachusetts Institute of Technology Press, Massachusetts, 1966.

————. "Estancia, Iloilo: Town in Transition," in *Modernization: Its Impact in the Philippines.* IPC Papers, No. 4. Ateneo de Manila University Press, Quezon City, 1967, 64–86.

Takahashi, Akira. *Land and Peasants in Central Luzon.* East-West Center Press, Honolulu, 1970, 196 pp. (This work uses a small village as a microcosm for the study of the socioeconomic structure of central Luzon village communities.)

Taylor, George Edward. *The Philippines and the United States: Problems of Partnership.* For the Council on Foreign Relations by Praeger, New York, 1964, 325 pp.

Taylor, D.M. and R.C. Gardner. "Roles of Stereotypes in Communication between Ethnic Groups in the Philippines." *Social Forces.* Vol. 49, December, 1970, 271–283.

Textor, Robert B. *Cultural Frontiers of the Peace Corps.* Massachusetts Institute of Technology Press, Massachusetts, 1966.

Thompson, R.E. "Missionary Dropouts—Is Leadership to Blame?" *World Vision Magazine.* February, 1966, 4 ff.

Tiryakian, Edward A. "The Prestige Evaluation of Occupations in an Underdeveloped Country: The Philippines." *American Journal of Sociology.* Vol. 63, No. 4, January, 1958, 390–399.

Tuggy, Arthur L. *The Philippine Church: Growth in a Changing Society.* William B. Eerdmans Publishing Company, Grand Rapids, Michigan, 1971, 191 pp.

———— and Ralph Toliver. *Seeing the Church in the Philippines.* O.M.F. Publishers, Manila, 1972, 172 pp.

U.S. International Cooperation Administration. *A Survey of Public Schools of the Philippines.* U.S. Operations Missions to the Philippines, Manila, 1960, 594 pp.

Vanderkroef, Justus M. "Patterns of Cultural Conflict in Philippine Life." *Pacific Affairs.* Fall and Winter, 1966, 326–338.

Vanoverbergh, M. *Dress and Adornment in the Mountain Province of Luzon, Philippine Islands.* Publication of the Catholic Anthropological Conference, 1929, Vol. 1, 181–242.

Varias, Rodolfo, R. "Psychiatry and the Filipino Personality." *Philippine Sociological Review*. Vol. 11, No. 3–4, July-October, 1963, 163–206.

Vayda, Andrew P. "Expansion and Warfare Among Swidden Agriculturists." *American Anthropologist*. Vol. 63, 1961, 346–358.

Villanueva, Buenaventura, M. et al. *Government and Administration of a Municipality*. Community Development Research Council, University of the Philippines, Quezon City, 1966.

Warriner, Charles K. "Myth and Reality in the Social Structure of the Philippines." *Philippine Sociological Review*. Vol. 8, No. 3–4, July-October, 1960, 26–32.

Waterman, G. Henry. "Problems of Syntax in the Translation of the Scriptures in Philippine Dialects." *The Bible Translator*. London, Vol. XI, No. 4, October, 1960, 162–172.

Webb, Eugene, et al. *Unobstrusive Measures: Nonreactive Research in the Social Sciences*. Rand McNally Company, Chicago, 1971, 42, 122–125.

Wernstedt, Frederick I. and J.E. Spencer. *The Philippine Island World: A Physical, Cultural, and Regional Geography*. University of California Press, Berkeley, 1967, 742 pp.

Whiting, Beatrice, ed. *Six Cultures: Studies on Child Rearing*. John Wiley and Sons, New York, 1963.

Whittemore, Lewis Bliss. *Struggle for Freedom: History of the Philippine Independent Church*. Seabury Press, Greenwich, Connecticut, 1961, 228.

Winter, Ralph. "The Planting of Younger Missions." *Church/Mission Tensions Today*. Edited by C. Peter Wagner. Moody Press, Chicago, 1972.

———. *Theological Education by Extension*. William Carey Library, Pasadena, 1969.

Wolff, Leon. *Little Brown Brothers*. Doubleday and Company, Garden City, New York, 1961, 366 pp. (A detailed and very readable account of how the United States claimed the Philippines at the turn of the century and imposed her control on Filipinos desiring self-rule. Wolff contends that the Filipinos were capable of governing themselves and that the U.S. was morally wrong in taking them. This is a must reading for North American missionaries to the Philippines.)

Wonderly, William L. and Eugene A. Nida. "Cultural Differences and the Community of Christian Values." *Practical Anthropology*. Vol. X, 1963, 241–258.

Worcester, Dean Conant. *The Philippines Past and Present*. The Macmillan Company, New York, 1930, 862 pp.

———. "The Non-Christian Tribes of the Philippines." *National Geographic*. Vol. 24, 1913, 1157–1256.

Yabes, Leopoldo Y. "Pilipino is not Filipino." *Solidarity*. Vol. 4, No. 2, February, 1969.

Zoebel, Fernando. *Philippine Religious Imagery*. Institute of Philippine Culture, Ateneo de Manila University Press, Quezon City, 154 pp.

LISTENING

(Selected audio materials)

Bayanihan On Tour. 12 inch, 33⅓ rpm, monaural or stereo, Monitor Records. (A recorded live performance of the Bayanihan Folk Arts Center's team of singers and dancers.)

Bayanihan Philippine Dance Company. 12 inch, 33⅓ rpm, monaural or stereo, two discs, Monitor Records. (Live performance recording.)

Bayanihan Sings! 12 inch, 33⅓ rpm, monaural or stereo, Monitor Records. (Songs of the Philippines.)

Case of the Bamboo-Sized Pigs in the album *Ways of Mankind*, Vol. 2, by Walter Goldschmidt, National Association of Education Broadcasters. (An anthropological study of law and justice among the Ifugao of the Philippines.)

Hanundo Music from the Philippines. 12 inch, 33⅓ rpm, monaural, two discs. Folkway and Scholastic Records, Scholastic Magazine, Englewood Cliffs, New Jersey.

Manila! Colorful Music of the Philippines. 12 inch, L.P., stereo, Capitol Records.

Music of the Magindanao in the Philippines. 12 inch, 33⅓ rpm, monaural, two discs. Folkway and Scholastic Records, Scholastic Magazine, Englewood Cliffs, New Jersey.

VIEWING

(Selected visual materials including films, film strips, and overhead transparencies)

Bayanihan. 16 mm., sound and color, 58 minutes. Produced by Robert Snyder, directed and written by Allegra Fuller Snyder. Bee Cross-Media, Rochester, New York, 1962. (The Bayanihan Philippine Dance Company survey the cultural history of the Philippines.)

Bayan Kong Filipinas. 16 mm., sound and color, 23 minutes. Palmer production. (The Philippines today from a Filipino point of view.)

The Cave People of the Philippines. 16 mm., sound and color, 39 minutes, TV Special, NBC, 1972. (The Lifestyle of the Tasady discovered in 1971.)

General Douglas MacArthur: "I Shall Return." 16 mm., sound, black and white, 15 minutes, A Star Film, adapted from the Fox Movitone News

Library. (General MacArthur's return to the Philippines during World War II.)

Hanunoo. 16 mm., color, music, no narration, 17 minutes, H.C. Conklin, 1958. (A study of the Hanunoo, farmers on Mindoro Island.)

The Last Tribes of Mindanao. 16 mm., sound and color, 52 minutes, TV Special, National Geographic, 1972.

Life of a Philippine Family. 16 mm., sound and color, 11 minutes, Coronet film 1957. (Daily life of a rural farm family on the island of Luzon.)

Muguindanao Kulintang Ensambles from Mindanao. 16 mm., sound and color, 16 minutes, Robert Garfias, ed., U.W. Pr. film, 1971. (Ethnic music and dance of Maguindanao of Northern Mindanao.)

Modern Indonesia and the Philippines. Filmstrip, color, 54 frames, S.V.E., 1962.

Music and Dance of the Bagobo and Manobo Peoples of Mindanao. 16 mm., sound and color, 12 minutes, Robert Garfias, ed. U.W. Pr., 1971, Bee-Cross Media. (Ethnic music and dance of Bogodo and Manobo people from west coast area of Gulf of Davao.)

Music and Dance of the Hill People of the Northern Philippines. 16 mm., sound and color, 29 minutes, Robert Garfias, ed., U.W. Pr., 1971, Bee-Cross Media.

Music and Dance of the Marano People of Mindanao. 16 mm., sound and color, 21 minutes, Robert Garfias, ed. U.W. Pr., 1971. Bee-Cross Media. (Ethnic music and dance of the Muslim Maranao people from the Lake Lanao Area.)

Music and Dance of the Yakan Peoples of Basilan Islands. 16 mm., sound and color, 12 minutes, Robert Garfias, ed. U.W. Pr., 1971, Bee-Cross Media. (Ethnic music and dance of the Muslim Yakans from the northernmost island of the Sulu Archipelago.)

"Overhead Transparencies on the Philippines." Bee-Cross Media, Rochester, New York. (Three series are available: Series One contains five sets of maps; Series Two contains transparencies on climate, seasons, resources and exports-imports; Series Three includes history, peoples, and cultural-linguistic groups.)

People of the Philippines. 16 mm., sound and color, 20 minutes. A Classroom Film Distributors production. (Deals with the Negritos, the Ifugaos, and the Muslim Moros.)

Philippines, The. 16 mm., sound, black and white, 15 minutes. Bee-Cross Media, Rochester, New York, 1953. (A U.S. Department of Defense film surveying the geography, peoples, and political history.)

Philippines: Gateway to the Far East. 16 mm., sound and color, 11 minutes. Coronet film, 1957. (Discusses the climate and geography of the Islands. Also illustrates Spanish and North American influence upon their way of life and optimistically presents their economic condition.)

Philippines, The: Island Republic. 16 mm., sound and color, 16 minutes. A McGraw-Hill film, 1968. (Presents the physical characteristics of the Islands, covering the three main regions: Luzon, Visaya, and Mindanao. Also optimistically presents the Philippine government and economy.)

Philippines, The: Land and People. 16 mm., sound and color, 14 minutes. Encyclopedia Britannica Educational Corporation film, 1959. (Shows the interrelationship between Philippine climate and geography on the one hand and the Filipino way of life on the other. Gives a historical survey of the influence of Spain and North America on the Islands and illustrates contemporary socioeconomic problems.)

Philippines, The: Nation of Islands. 16 mm., sound and color, 17 minutes. United World Film, 1962. (An introduction to the nation of the Republic of the Philippines. Surveys life in various parts of the country including Manila, Cebu, Maotan and Mindanao. Contains a nationalistic emphasis upon "progress.")

Philippines Today, The. 16 mm., sound and color, 20 minutes. A Classroom Film Distributors production, 1958. (Describes the life of the Filipino in Manila, the Mountain Province, Jolo and Zamboanga.)

Republic of the Philippines, The. 16 mm., sound and color, 18 minutes. Dudley Pictures; Universal Educational and Visual Arts, 1959. (An introduction to the Philippines including a survey of physical geography, agriculture, natural resources, peoples, and contrast in community forms.)

Rice Growing in Bontoc. Color Filmstrip, 71 frames, Ronald Wilcox, B.C.I.M., 1972.

Samal Dances from Taluksangay. 16 mm., sound and color, 12 minutes, Robert Garfias, ed. U.W. Pr., 1971, Bee-Cross Media. (Ethnic music and dance from village of Taluksangay on the island of Mindanao.)

GAMING

(Simulation games and structured experiences)

Overpower. Associates of Urbanus, Box 457, Farmington, Michigan. (A simulation of the North American class stratification system.)

Strata. Associates of Urbanus, Box 457, Farmington, Michigan. (A simulation of the Filipino status stratification system.)

Publications of the
INTERNATIONAL MUSEUM OF CULTURES

1. SARAYACU QUICHUA POTTERY by Patricia Kelley and Carolyn Orr, 1976.
   (Also available in Spanish as CERAMICA QUICHUA DE SARAYACU.) $ 3.00

2. A LOOK AT LATIN AMERICAN LIFESTYLES by Marvin Mayers, 1976. $ 6.45

3. COGNITIVE STUDIES OF SOUTHERN MESOAMERICA by Helen Neuenswander and
   Dean Arnold, eds., 1977. (Also available in Spanish as ESTUDIOS
   COGNITIVOS DEL SUR DE MESOAMERICA.) $10.95

4. THE DRAMA OF LIFE: GUAMBIANO LIFE CYCLE CUSTOMS by Judith Branks and
   Juan Bautista Sánchez, 1978. $ 5.00

5. THE USARUFAS AND THEIR MUSIC by Vida Chenoweth, 1979. $14.90

6. NOTES FROM INDOCHINA: ON ETHNIC MINORITY CULTURES by Marilyn
   Gregerson and Dorothy Thomas, eds., 1980. $ 9.45

7. THE DENI OF WESTERN BRAZIL: A STUDY OF SOCIOPOLITICAL ORGANIZATION AND
   COMMUNITY DEVELOPMENT by Gordon Koop and Sherwood G. Lingenfelter, 1980.
   (Also available in Portuguese as OS DENI DO BRASIL OCIDENTAL--UM ES-
   TUDO DE ORGANIZACAO SOCIO-POLITICA E DESENVOLVIMENTO COMUNITARIO.) $ 5.95

8. A LOOK AT FILIPINO LIFESTYLES by Marvin Mayers, 1980. $ 8.45

9. NUEVO DESTINO: THE LIFE STORY OF A SHIPIBO BILINGUAL EDUCATOR
   by Lucille Eakin, 1980. $ 2.95

10. A MIXTEC LIME OVEN by Kenneth L. Pike, 1980. $ 1.25

11. PROTO OTOMANGUEAN KINSHIP by William R. Merrifield, 1981. (Also
    available in Spanish as PARENTESCO PROTO OTOMANGUE.) $12.50

12. PEOPLE OF UCAYALI: THE SHIPIBO AND CONIBO OF PERU by Lucille Eakin,
    Erwin Lauriault, and Harry Boonstra, in preparation. $--.--

13. STICKS AND STRAW: COMPARATIVE HOUSE FORMS IN SOUTHERN SUDAN AND
    NORTHERN KENYA by Jonathan E. Arensen, 1983. $12.00

14. GRAFTING OLD ROOTSTOCK ed. by Philip A. Noss. $10.95

15. A VIEW FROM THE ISLANDS: THE SAMAL OF TAWI-TAWI by Karen J. Allison. $--.--

17. GODS, HEROES, KINSMEN: ETHNOGRAPHIC STUDIES FROM IRIAN JAYA,
    INDONESIA ed. by William R. Merrifield, Marilyn Gregerson, and
    Daniel C. Ajamiseba. $15.00

These titles are available at

The International Museum of Cultures
7500 W. Camp Wisdom Road
Dallas, Texas   75236

Residents of Texas add 5% sales tax.